fantastic floorcloths
you can paint in a day

Judy Diephouse & Lynne Deptula

NORTH LIGHT BOOKS

Cincinnati, Ohio
www.artistsnetwork.com

Fantastic Floorcloths You Can Paint in a Day.
Copyright © 2005 by Judy Diephouse and Lynne Deptula. Manufactured in China. All rights reserved. The patterns and drawings in this book are for the personal use of the decorative painter. By permission of the authors and publisher, they may be either hand-traced or photocopied to make single copies, but under no circumstances may they be resold or republished. It is permissible for the purchaser to paint the designs contained herein and sell them at fairs, bazaars, and craft shows. No other part of this book may be reproduced in any form or by any electronic or mechanical means including information storage and retrieval systems without permission in writing from the publisher, except by a reviewer, who may quote brief passages in a review. The content of this book has been thoroughly reviewed for accuracy. However, the authors and publisher disclaim any liability for any damages, losses or injuries that may result from the use or misuse of any product or information presented herein. It is the purchaser's responsibility to read and follow all instructions and warnings on all product labels. Published by North Light Books, an imprint of F+W Publications, Inc., 4700 East Galbraith Road, Cincinnati, Ohio 45236. (800) 289-0963. First edition.

Other fine North Light Books are available from your local bookstore, art supply store or direct from the publisher.

09 08 07 06 05   5 4 3 2 1

Library of Congress Cataloging-in-Publication Data

Diephouse, Judy
    Fantastic floorcloths you can paint in a day / Judy Diephouse & Lynne Deptula.
      p. cm.
    ISBN 1-58180-603-5 (pbk.)
    1. Painting. w. Floor coverings. I. Deptula, Lynne, II. Title.

TT385.D543 2005
747'.4--dc22

2004057571

fw

F+W PUBLICATIONS, INC.

Editor: Holly Davis
Production Coordinator: Kristen Heller
Art Director: Camille DeRhodes
Interior Layout Artist: Kathy Gardner
Photographer: Christine Polomsky and Hal Barkan
Photo Stylist: Nora Martini

metric conversion chart

to convert	to	multiply by
Inches	Centimeters	2.54
Centimeters	Inches	0.4
Feet	Centimeters	30.5
Centimeters	Feet	0.03
Yards	Meters	0.9
Meters	Yards	1.1
Sq. Inches	Sq. Centimeters	6.45
Sq. Centimeters	Sq. Inches	0.16
Sq. Feet	Sq. Meters	0.09
Sq. Meters	Sq. Feet	10.8
Sq. Yards	Sq. Meters	0.8
Sq. Meters	Sq. Yards	1.2
Pounds	Kilograms	0.45
Kilograms	Pounds	2.2
Ounces	Grams	28.3
Grams	Ounces	0.035

about the authors

Judy Diephouse

Lynn Deptula

Judy Diephouse and Lynne Deptula both reside in the Grand Rapids, Michigan, area with their families. Having been business partners for more than 20 years, they truly love designing and teaching decorative painting. They feel they have been blessed to have a job that is so inspiring, stimulating and just plain fun. Lynne and Judy travel teach at decorative painting conventions and seminars throughout the United States. They have designed more than 250 pattern packets and 20 books, including *Painting Blooms and Blossoms*, *Folk Art Landscapes for Every Season* and *Painting Your Flea Market Finds*. Visit their Web site to view the latest selections of pattern packets and books, pick up a few painting tips and download a free pattern. Their Web address is www.distinctivebrushstrokes.com

Lynne Deptula
7245 Cascade Woods Drive SE
Grand Rapids, MI 49546
Phone-616-940-1899
Fax-616-940-6002
E-mail-dbrush1@aol.com

Judy Diephouse
9796 Myers Lake Ave. NE
Rockford, MI 49341
Phone-616-874-1656
Fax-616-874-1713
E-mail-distinctj@aol.com

contents

introduction

Handpainted floorcloths are a hot decorating trend. If you've looked at home décor magazines or gone through decorator design homes, you'll have noticed handpainted floorcloths of all sizes. In this book we hope to inspire you to make these delightful accents for your own home or as gifts for family and friends. We've included designs for a variety of rooms in your home and designs for various seasons of the year. We encourage you to paint several—they're fun, easy to do and easy to store. What's more, they're painted on an inexpensive surface.

If you've never painted floorcloths, you'll be pleased with how easy they are to prep, paint and finish. They're also very easy to care for after completed. Once you've applied two or three coats of acrylic varnish, you can easily clean them with a soft cloth and mild soap.

A few projects in this book, such as Whimsical Flower (page 18), Field of Daisies (page 80) and Stars and Stripes (page 88), make great family projects. Try them with your children or grandchildren.

As a bonus, we adapted several of our designs to accessory pieces, so you can see how easy it is to coordinate these floorcloths with other items. We hope seeing our accessory ideas inspires you to paint your own coordinated décor accents.

Have Fun and Happy Painting,
Judy Diephouse and Lynne Deptula

materials

chapter 1

You can create beautiful floorcloths with the basic painting supplies listed on these two pages. More specific material lists are included with each project. These materials should be readily available in your local hobby or craft store, but if you have trouble finding an item, see Resources on page 126 for help.

paints

We used Delta Ceramcoat paints in this book. They're nontoxic, water-based acrylics sold in bottles. Shake the bottle well before using to make sure the binder is mixed with the pigments. These paints can be thinned with water for a more transparent look or to achieve an ink-like consistency for strokework.

brushes

All brushes used in this book are from Loew-Cornell. See the types used on the right.

Deerfoot stippler (series 7850)
Liner (series 7350)
Script liner (series 7050)
Jackie Shaw liner (series JS)
Mop (series 275)
Shader (series 7300)
Rake (series 7120)
Wash (series 7150 or 7550)
Round stroke (series 7040)

surfaces

Most projects in this book are painted on Fredrix pre-primed floor-cloth canvas. Look for them in the stretched canvas area of your hobby or craft store. They come in a variety of shapes and sizes, the most common size being 2' x 3' (61cm x 91cm).

If you want to paint bigger cloths, you can cut the size you need from a large roll. For canvas floorcloth tips and care, see page 8. Two of our designs are painted on sisal rugs, which we purchased from a home decor store.

general supplies

Round out your painting materials with these items:

sponge roller A 2- to 4-inch (51mm to 102mm) sponge roller is great for basecoating large areas.

tracing paper Thin paper used to trace a pattern after it has been enlarged to the appropriate percentage, if necessary.

graphite paper This paper is used to transfer the traced pattern onto the floorcloth. It comes in gray, black, and white.

stylus A good stylus is useful in applying the pattern to the project and for any fine dots and details you add to the painting. Often a stylus comes with points on both ends, one smaller than the other.

quilter's ruler This clear plastic ruler has markings on both its length and width, which makes it a perfect tool for marking borders or grids.

pencils Always have a supply of sharpened no. 2 graphite, chalk pencils, or soapstone pencils in your paint supplies. When tracing a pattern, a small area may be omitted. Instead of trying to reposition the pattern exactly, you can freehand the extra detail.

water basin Many brands of water basins are available. A good basin will have ridges across one section of the bottom. Pull your brush ferrule (metal part) across the ridges to loosen and remove the paint on your brush. Grooves on the other side of the basin will hold your brushes in the water, which prevents the paint from drying in your brush. A high divider in the basin helps keep the supply of clean water on one side.

palette We use disposable waxed palettes. We do not use wet palettes, because we often blend colors on the brush before painting. If the palette is wet, the brush will pick up the moisture and create difficulty in achieving a nice gradual blend.

palette knife A palette knife comes in handy when you need to mix paints.

tape We recommend blue painter's tape for masking off borders on the floorcloths. Place the tape where you need it, then seal the edge with your finger. (See Preventing Bleeding Under Masking Tape on page 12.)

sponge and sponge sheets A small round sponge is used for painting clouds and foliage. Sponge sheets can be cut into shapes for stenciling.

toothbrush An old toothbrush is the best tool for spattering and flyspecking See page 12 for instructions.

fine-point permanent black ink pen Used for adding outlines, crosshatching and other design details.

eraser A brown gum eraser is great for removing pencil markings or graphite transfer lines.

varnish We recommend finishing the canvas floorcloths with Delta Ceramcoat Satin Interior Varnish and the sisal mats with Delta Ceramcoat Matte Interior Spray Varnish. See page 13 for more information.

techniques & tips

The procedures, brush loads, strokes and tips explained in this chapter aren't complicated, but they can make all the difference in your painting. Get familiar with the terminology. Practice the loads and strokes. As you work on a particular project, refer back to this material as necessary. The extra time you take will pay off big in your finished floorcloths.

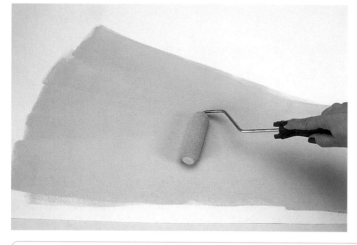

surface basecoating

Generally you'll begin your floorcloth painting with a surface basecoat applied with a sponge roller. First squeeze an even amount of paint around the cloth. Then roll out the paint evenly. You may need to add a second coat with darker colors.

tracing and transferring patterns

Enlarge your project pattern to the specified percentage. Copy this pattern onto tracing paper. Place graphite paper, coated side down, between the tracing-paper pattern and the painting surface. Press along the pattern lines with a stylus. If necessary, move the pattern and graphite paper to repeat a motif.

canvas tips

1) Rolled floorcloth canvas gets tight, especially when it's cold. Use a hair dryer as you gradually unroll the cloth after you first take it out of the packaging tube. Do the same when you unroll a finished, stored floorcloth to avoid cracking the paint. 2) Floorcloth canvas is easy to cut into any shape you wish. 3) Fredrix floorcloth canvas is primed with gesso by the manufacturer twice on one side and once on the other. The side with two coatings is smoother and may be preferred by beginners because it's easier to paint. Some painters prefer the other side for its more visible texture. You may even decide to paint one design on one side and another on the other side. 4) Canvas floorcloths last for years, but as they get older, the corners may curl a bit. To remedy this problem, cut rounded corners. You can get a consistent curve by tracing along a juice glass

creating rounded corners

double load and double-loaded stroke

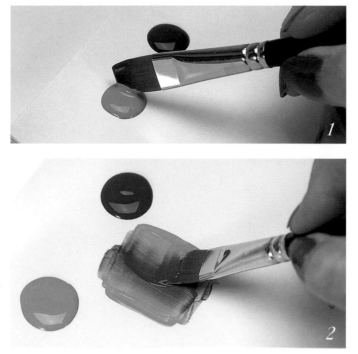

1 Dip one side of the brush in the first color and the other side into the second color.

2 Blend well on the palette to achieve a gradual gradation of color. Make sure to blend both sides of the brush.

side load and side-load float

1 Dip one side of a slightly dampened brush into the paint.

2 Blend on the palette until you get strong color on one side of the stroke that gradually fades to nothing on the other side. This gradual shading is called a float.

3 For a softer float, wet your painting surface with clean water. Stroke the float and soften with a mop brush.

tipping

1 Load both sides of the brush with the first color.

2 Tip the brush into the second color.

3 Here is a stroke made with a tipped brush.

lifeline

A lifeline is a wavy trim line that divides sections of your painting. To paint a lifeline, weave back and forth with a script liner.

s-stroke

Start on the chisel edge, press to the right as you pull down and rise to the chisel as you pull left. In this photo I'm using a shader brush (also called a flat), but you can also use a round. A series of these strokes can create a border.

comma stroke

Press the loaded brush down for the stroke head. Rise gradually to the chisel as you pull the stroke tail. In this photo I'm using a shader brush (also called a flat), but you can also use a round.

lifeline tip

The term "lifeline" comes from folk art painters who thought of it as depicting the ups and downs of life.

petal stroke

This stroke can be made with a double- or side-loaded brush. Start the chisel edge on one side of the petal, press down as you cross the top of the petal and lift to the chisel as you come to the opposite side of the petal.

chisel petal stroke

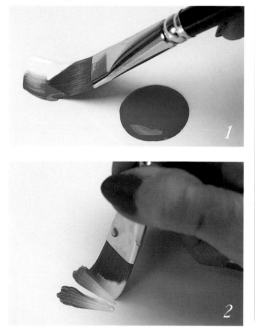

1 Start with a double-loaded brush, slightly blended on the palette.

2 Stand on the chisel edge of the brush and wiggle it back and forth to create the petal, returning to the chisel edge of the brush on the other side of the petal.

one-stroke leaf

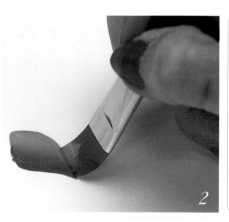

1 Hold the brush at a slight angle.

2 Press the brush down, quickly bring it to the chisel edge and slide off. Don't turn the brush. This photo shows a leaf made with a double-loaded brush, but you can use any type of load.

flyspecking

1 Dip a toothbrush into water. Then load the toothbrush with paint and work it out a bit. The thinner the paint, the larger the flyspecking dots.

2 Hold the bristles up and scrape over their tops with your index fingernail. The harder you press, the larger the spray.

checking

1 Always start the first check in the outside corner. Place the second check at the corner of the first check.

2 As you continue checking, avoid letting the corners touch so you can adjust the spacing as needed. For a nice square check, stay on the chisel edge of the brush.

preventing bleeding under masking tape

When you're painting a stripe, masking tape helps you achieve straight lines, as long as the paint doesn't bleed under the tape. To sidestep this problem, seal your tape with the basecoat color before you use the stripe color. If the basecoat color bleeds, it will match the surface.

sponge shape stippling

1 With a sponge sheet, you can easily stipple any shape. Trace the desired shape on the sponge sheet and cut it out.

2 Soak the sponge-sheet shape in water to expand the fibers. You can do this in a tub of water or under the faucet, but don't use your brush basin. Squeeze out the excess moisture with a paper towel.

3 Dab the sponge shape into the paint and pounce out the excess on a paper towel.

4 When you have the desired paint saturation, go ahead with your sponge stippling.

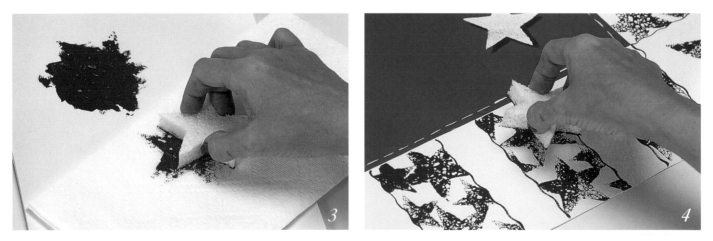

varnishing

When the painting on your canvas floorcloth is dry, apply two to three coats of Delta Ceramcoat Satin Interior Varnish with a large flat or mop brush. After these coats dry, apply a coat to the underside. This will help keep the mat from curling and also prevent water from seeping into the painting from the bottom.

To protect the painting on sisal rugs, lightly mist the painted areas with Delta Ceramcoat Matte Interior Spray Varnish.

always-in-season floorcloths

Once you paint one floorcloth and find how easy and fun it is, you'll just have to

paint more! In this section we've included designs that look great all year long—

although we're guessing you'll enjoy trading them off once in a while, just for vari-

ety. Projects like the Whimsical Flower mat are perfect for decorative painters, young

and older, who are just starting out. If you have some decorative painting experience,

you know the appeal of floral designs, and the Floral Fancy and Blue Strokes floor-

cloths are just two of many wonderful florals you have to choose from. Floorcloths

are so inexpensive to paint and make such wonderful gifts, we know you won't be

able stop with just one. So enjoy the whole distinctive collection!

checks and flowers

Perhaps you're one of the many of us who love the decorating look of yellow, white and blue. While I was designing this project, I knew the exact spot in my guest bedroom where this floorcloth would look great. But if the colors don't fit your taste or décor, you can easily change to another color combination.

colors
paint (Delta Ceramcoat)

light ivory	mello yellow	blue heaven	toffee brown
forest green	sea grass	white	blue jay
eucalyptus	eucalyptus + white (1:1) thinned with water		

materials
surface
Fredrix floorcloth canvas, 2' x 3' (61cm x 91cm)

brushes (Loew-Cornell)
Wash, series 7150 or 7550: ½-inch (13mm), 1-inch (25mm), 1½-inch (38mm) ~ Shader, series 7300: no. 8 ~ Deerfoot stippler, series 7850: ¼-inch (6mm) ~ Script liner, series 7050: no. 1

additional supplies
2- to 4-inch (51mm to 102mm) sponge roller ~ Pencil ~ Quilter's ruler ~ Tracing paper ~ Dark graphite paper and stylus ~ Brown gum eraser ~ Delta Ceramcoat Satin Interior Varnish ~ Large flat or mop brush for varnishing

(pattern for this floorcloth is on page 114)

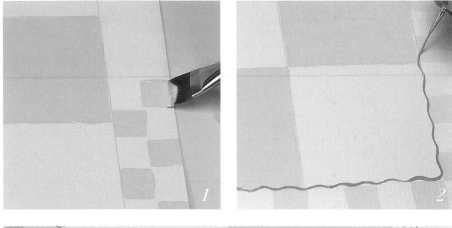

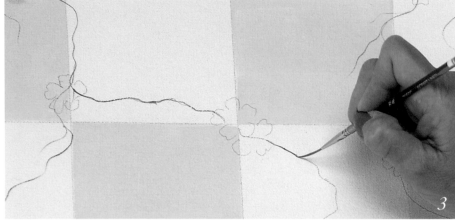

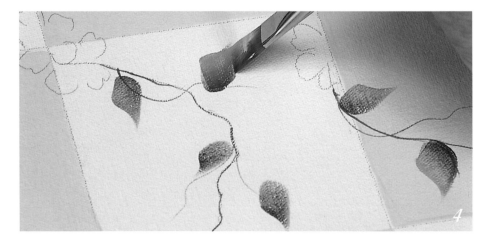

1 basecoat floorcloth and paint checks

Basecoat the entire cloth with Light Ivory, using a sponge roller. Mark off a 2-inch (5.1cm) outside border with a pencil and quilter's ruler. Then measure and mark 4-inch (10.2cm) checks inside the border. Paint alternate checks with one coat of Mello Yellow, using a 1½-inch (38mm) wash. Next paint the outside checks in the same color with a 1-inch (25mm) wash. Start the checks in the corners and work toward the middle. Adjust spacing so the checks meet in the middle of a side.

2 add a lifeline

Paint the lifeline between the border and the middle area with Blue Heaven, using a no. 1 script liner.

3 paint tendrils

The design can be painted freehand or with a pattern. If you're using the pattern, repeat the design in the middle area. Paint tendrils with Toffee Brown, using a no. 1 script liner.

4 stroke in larger leaves

Double load the ½-inch (13mm) wash with Forest Green and Sea Grass. Blend thoroughly on your palette to achieve a gradual gradation of color. Using the one-stroke leaf technique (see page 11), paint the larger leaves.

5 stroke in flowers and buds

Double load a no. 8 shader into White and Blue Heaven or White and Blue Jay. Using two blues allows tone variation, but use one combination per flower. Paint the flowers with petal strokes (see page 11). Buds are smaller petal strokes.

6 stipple in flower centers

Using a ¼-inch (6mm) deerfoot, lightly stipple in the flower centers with Mello Yellow. Touch the brush toe (longest bristles) into Toffee Brown and stipple shading on one side of the centers. With the no. 1 script liner, add a White highlight, such as you see on the left flower.

7 add shadow leaves

Brush-mix Eucalyptus + White (1:1), thinned with water. Using a no. 8 shader, paint the shadow leaves using the one-stroke leaf technique. Allow the floorcloth to dry thoroughly. Erase any visible tracing lines with a brown gum eraser and then varnish (see page 13).

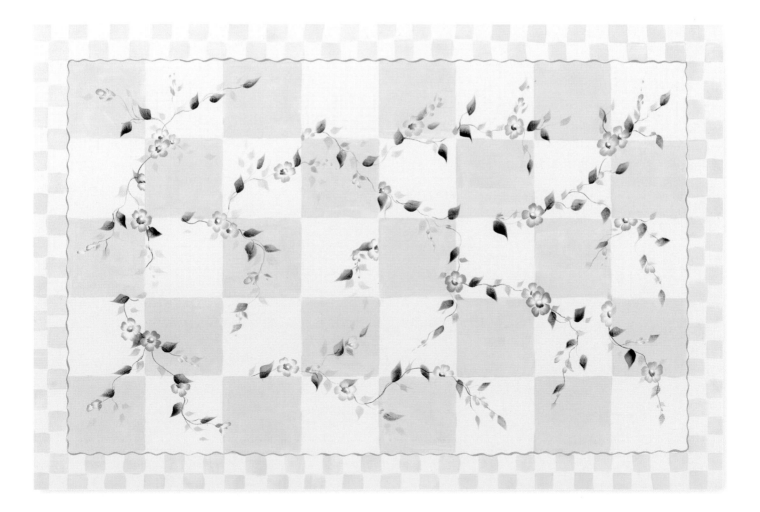

whimsical flower

Place this floorcloth in a bedroom, bathroom or in front of the kitchen sink to bring a little sunshine to each day. Create a special memory by painting it with a child and customizing the colors to that child's room. Then use these design ideas to create custom accessories, such as the tissue box holder and catch-all box on the opposite page.

materials

surface
Fredrix floorcloth canvas, 2' x 3' (61cm x 91cm)

brushes (Loew-Cornell)
Wash, series 7150 or 7550: ¾-inch (19mm) ~ Shader, series 7300: nos. 4 & 8 ~ Rake, series 7120: ½-inch (13mm) ~ Jackie Shaw liner, series JS: no. 1 ~ Script liner, series 7050: no. 4

additional supplies
Tracing paper ~ Dark graphite paper and stylus ~ Household scissors ~ 2- to 4-inch (51mm to 102mm) sponge roller ~ Pencil ~ Straightedge ~ Compass ~ Brown gum eraser ~ Delta Ceramcoat Satin Interior Varnish ~ Large flat or mop brush for varnishing

(pattern for this floorcloth is on page 114)

colors
paint (Delta Ceramcoat)

candlelight	caribbean blue	white	pink quartz
island coral	coastline blue	village green	pale lilac

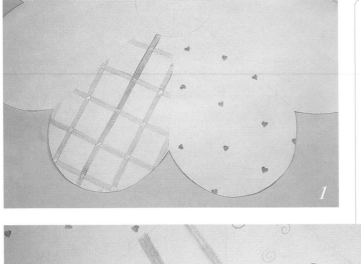

1 cut shape, basecoat and detail first two petals

Transfer the flower pattern onto the floorcloth. Cut out the flower shape, using household scissors. Basecoat the entire surface with two coats of Candlelight on a sponge roller, letting the paint dry between coats. Using a straightedge and pencil, draw lines between each flower petal, crossing the entire canvas. Using a compass, lightly mark a 4½" (11cm) flower center. Start with the blue plaid section. Load a no. 8 shader with thinned Caribbean Blue. Paint freehand vertical lines outward to the edge of the petal. Let dry. Paint horizontal lines across the vertical. Let dry. Detail the squares at the intersections of the horizontal and vertical lines with tiny diagonal lines, using a no. 1 Jackie Shaw liner and White.

On the second petal section, paint little freehand hearts, using a no. 1 Jackie Shaw liner and Pink Quartz. Scatter the hearts around the section.

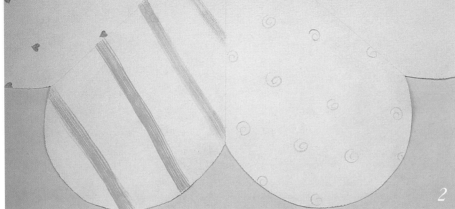

2 detail third and fourth petals

Detail the third petal section with diagonal lines painted with a ½-inch (13mm) rake and thinned Island Coral.

Now detail the fourth petal section with randomly placed spirals of Coastline Blue painted with a no. 1 Jackie Shaw liner.

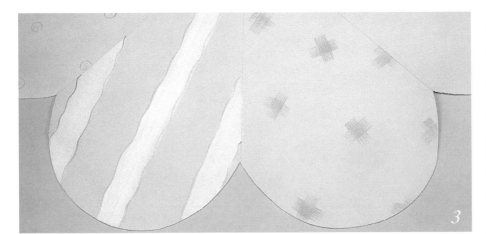

3 detail fifth and sixth petals

Detail the fifth petal section with vertical stripes painted with a ¾-inch (19mm) wash and thinned White. Outline both edges of each White stripe with a wavy lifeline of Caribbean Blue. Use a no. 1 Jackie Shaw liner.

Now detail the sixth petal section with randomly scattered crisscrosses painted with Village Green on a ½-inch (13mm) rake.

4 detail seventh and eighth petals

Detail the seventh petal section with vertical rick-rack lines of thinned Pink Quartz on a no. 4 shader.

For the last petal section, scatter random White polka dots painted with the handle end of any paint brush.

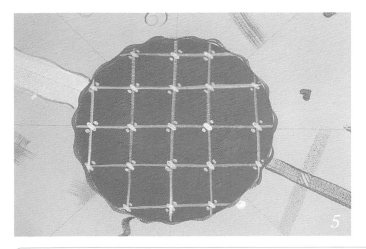

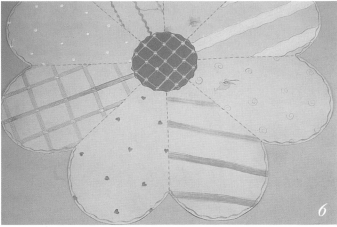

5 paint the flower center

Basecoat the flower center with Pale Lilac on a ¾-inch (19mm) wash. Paint the crisscross linework in the flower center with thinned White and a no. 1 Jackie Shaw liner. Then with the same brush, detail each linework intersection with one dash line flanked by two smaller dashes of White. Around the edge of the flower center, paint a wavy lifeline with thinned Caribbean Blue on the no. 1 Jackie Shaw liner.

6 add stitch lines and lifelines

Finish the flower mat with painted stitching lines between each flower petal. Use thinned Village Green and a no. 4 script liner. Paint a wavy lifeline around the outside edge of the flower mat with thinned Village Green on the same brush. Allow the floorcloth to dry completely. Erase any visible pattern lines with a brown gum eraser and then varnish (see page 13).

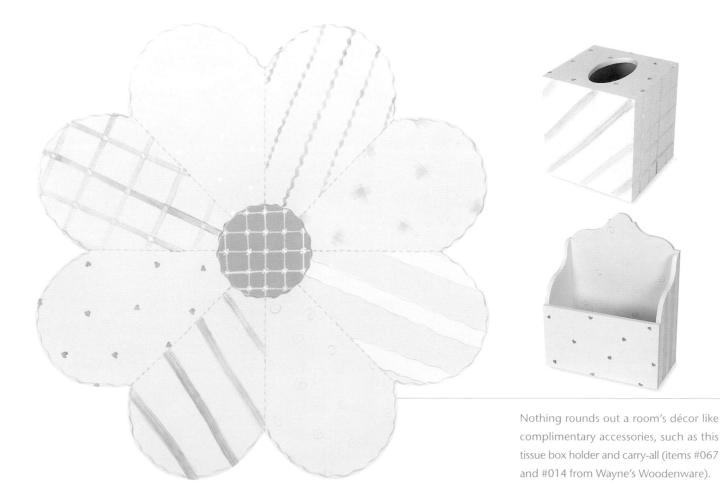

Nothing rounds out a room's décor like complimentary accessories, such as this tissue box holder and carry-all (items #067 and #014 from Wayne's Woodenware).

fresh fruit

We love this "patchwork" style of painting designs. You can fill the patches with these great fruit stencils or get extra creative and use other stencils that coordinate with an existing decorated space. If you can't find a stencil in the shape you want, just make your own (see page 39).

colors
paint (Delta Ceramcoat)

raw linen	stonewedge green	golden brown	burnt sienna
sunbright yellow	fuchsia	black cherry	moroccan red
	bright yellow	dark forest green	

materials

surface
Fredrix floorcloth canvas, 2' x 3' (61cm x 91cm)

brushes (Loew-Cornell)
Wash, series 7150 or 7550: 1-inch (25mm) ~ Deerfoot stippler, series 7850: ½-inch (13mm) ~ Script liner, series 7050: no. 4

additional supplies
2- to 4-inch (51mm to 102mm) sponge roller ~ Pencil ~ Quilter's ruler ~ Masking tape ~ Clear Con-Tact paper ~ Delta Stencil Magic "Beautiful Fruits" stencil ~ Round craft sponge ~ Fine-point permanent black ink pen ~ Brown gum eraser ~ Delta Ceramcoat Matte Interior Spray Varnish ~ Delta Ceramcoat Satin Interior Varnish ~ Large flat or mop brush for final varnishing

(this floorcloth is painted without patterns)

1 basecoat, mask and basecoat again

Basecoat the entire floorcloth with Raw Linen on a sponge roller. Measure and mark off a 2½" (6.4cm) border around the floorcloth. Tape off this border area with masking tape. Cut Con-Tact paper for the squares as follows: cherries are 4" x 6" (10.2cm x 15.2cm); apples are 5" x 6" (12.7cm x 15.2cm); pears are 5½" x 6" (14.0cm x 15.2cm). Peel off the Con-Tact paper backing and stick the rectangles in a random arrangement on the field of the floorcloth. Paint over the field and the Con-Tact paper squares with Stonewedge Green on a sponge roller. Let dry and then peel off the Con-Tact paper.

2 base and shade pear

Place the pear stencil over a 5½" x 6" (14.0cm x 15.2cm) square and tape it down with masking tape. Also mask the leaf and stem cutouts. Load the curve of a round craft sponge with Golden Brown and stencil in the pear's basecoat color. While the paint is still wet, load Burnt Sienna on a small curve of the sponge and shade the pear's left side.

3 highlight the pear

While the paint is still wet, load Sunbright Yellow on a small curve of the sponge and highlight the center of the pear. Repeat steps 2 and 3 for all other pear squares.

4 stencil the cherries

Place the cherry stencil on a 4" x 6" (10.2cm x 15.2cm) square, tape it down and mask off the leaf and stem stencil cutouts. Using a ½-inch (13mm) deerfoot stipple brush loaded into Fuchsia, stipple on the cherry basecoat. While the basecoat is still wet, side load the brush with Black Cherry and shade one side of each cherry. Repeat for all other cherry squares.

5 stencil the apples

Place the apple stencil on a 5" x 6" (12.7cm x 15.2cm) square, tape it down and mask off the leaf and stem cutouts. Using the round craft sponge, basecoat stipple the apple with Moroccan Red. While the basecoat is still wet, side load the craft sponge into Black Cherry and shade one side of the apple. Again working wet into wet, side load the craft sponge into Bright Yellow and stipple the apple's highlight. Repeat for all other apple squares.

6 stencil all leaves

Stencil the leaves on the pears, apples and cherries with Dark Forest Green on a ½-inch (13mm) deerfoot stipple brush. Let the green fade out toward the top edges of the leaves. Highlight with Bright Yellow along some of the leaf top edges and tips.

7 paint stems and square outlines

Stencil in the apple and pear stems with Dark Forest Green. Then come back in with Black Cherry to shade. The cherry stems are stenciled with a mix of these two colors to make a brown shade. The outlines on each square are painted with a no. 4 script liner. Use Fuchsia to outline the cherry squares, Golden Brown to outline the pears and Black Cherry to outline the apple squares.

8 ink in stitching lines and paint checks

With a fine-point permanent black ink pen, detail with "stitching lines" around the perimeter of each square and around the fruits. Ink some bows and ribbons on random corners of the fruit squares. Then ink stitching lines of fruit shapes scattered on the green floorcloth background. Paint a checkerboard design in the four corners of the floorcloth, using thinned Black Cherry on a 1-inch (25mm) wash. Allow the floorcloth to dry completely and then erase visible pencil lines with a brown gum eraser. Now mist the ink markings with Delta Ceramcoat Matte Interior Spray Varnish to prevent the ink from bleeding when you brush varnish the entire mat (see page 13).

urban squares

Here's a design for urban-styled homes—bold, geometric and sure to add that punch of color where it's needed! Painting square pillows with this same technique is easy. Just add a touch of fabric medium to each acrylic color to make the paint bind to the fabric.

materials

surface
Fredrix floorcloth canvas, 2' x 3' (61cm x 91cm)

brushes (Loew-Cornell)
Script liner, series 7050: no. 4

additional supplies
2- to 4-inch (51mm to 102mm)
sponge roller ~ Quilter's ruler ~ Chalk pencil ~
Sponge squares: 5" (13cm), 4" (10cm), 2" (5cm) ~
Brown gum eraser ~ Delta Ceramcoat
Satin Interior Varnish ~ Large flat
or mop brush for varnishing

(this floorcloth is painted without patterns)

colors

paint (Delta Ceramcoat)

espresso   light foliage green   purple smoke   empire gold

caribbean blue   golden brown   periwinkle blue   latte

1 basecoat, divide into sections and sponge six squares

Basecoat the canvas floorcloth with Espresso and a sponge roller. Let dry. Using a quilter's ruler and a chalk pencil, divide the floorcloth into a grid of 6" (15cm) squares. Load a dampened 5" (13cm) square sponge with Light Foliage Green and press it onto your waxed palette to remove excess paint. Then press the sponge into the center of six randomly selected grid squares, reloading with paint as necessary.

2 continue sponging squares

Rinse the 5" (13cm) square sponge in clear water and wring it out until damp. Load into Purple Smoke and press the sponge into the center of six randomly selected unsponged squares. Rinse the sponge again, load with Empire Gold and press the sponge into the center of another six randomly selected un-sponged squares. Let dry completely.

Using a dampened 4" (10cm) square sponge, load into Caribbean Blue and sponge a square in the middle of the 5" (13cm) Light Foliage Green squares. Rinse the 4" (10cm) sponge, load into Golden Brown and add a square in the middle of each 5" (13cm) Purple Smoke square. In the same manner, add a 4" (10cm) Periwinkle Blue square in the middle of each 5" (13cm) Empire Gold square. Let all the paint dry.

3 keep sponging squares

Load a dampened 2" (5cm) sponge into Purple Smoke and sponge an off-center square in each 4" (10cm) Caribbean Blue square. Rinse the sponge, load in Light Foliage Green and add an off-center square in each 4" (10cm) Golden Brown square. In the same manner, add a 2" (5cm) off-center Caribbean Blue square in each 4" (10cm) Periwinkle Blue square.

sponge tip

You may prefer to cut a sponge square of appropriate size for each color rather than rinsing the squares before color changes.

4 paint "maze" lines

Fill the remaining empty squares with a linework "maze" painted with thinned Latte and a no. 4 script liner. The lines of the maze should be about 3⁄4" (19mm) apart. Leave the beginning and end of the maze open. The outside end of the maze is finished with a short line drawn away from the maze. Allow the floorcloth to dry completely. Remove any visible chalk pencil lines with a brown gum eraser and then varnish (see page 13).

The Urban Squares floorcloth design works well in a family or living room—a place where people relax. Matching pillows are a natural.

floral fancy

This is a fun and easy floorcloth to do. The black-line finishing detail, which adds so much, is done with a fine-point permanent pen. We recommend that any time you use a permanent pen, you lightly mist the ink with Delta Ceramcoat Matte Interior Spray Varnish. This will prevent any accidental bleeding of the ink.

colors
paint (Delta Ceramcoat)

candlelight	medium foliage green	dark foliage green	light foliage green
sunbright yellow	antique gold	white	purple dusk
blue jay	indiana rose	wild rose	peony
pale lilac	lilac	deep lilac	sunbright yellow + antique gold (1:1)

materials

surface
Fredrix floorcloth canvas, 2' x 3' (61cm x 91cm)

brushes (Loew-Cornell)
Wash, series 7150 or 7550: 1-inch (25mm) ~ Shader, series 7300: nos. 2, 8, 12, 16, & 20 ~ Round stroke, series 7040: no. 6 ~ Jackie Shaw liner, series JS: no. 1

additional supplies
2- to 4-inch (51mm to 102mm) sponge roller ~ Pencil ~ Quilter's ruler ~ Tracing paper ~ Dark graphite paper and stylus ~ Fine-point permanent black ink pen ~ Brown gum eraser~ Delta Ceramcoat Matte Interior Spray Varnish ~ Delta Ceramcoat Satin Interior Varnish ~ Large flat or mop brush for final varnishing

(patterns for this floorcloth are on page 115)

1 base, transfer, paint leaves and stems

Basecoat the entire cloth with Candlelight, using a sponge roller. Let dry. Mark off a 2-inch (5cm) border with a ruler and pencil. Transfer the flower shapes randomly onto the inner panel. Paint the stems with Medium Foliage Green, using a no. 1 Jackie Shaw liner. Load a no. 12 shader with Medium Foliage Green, touching into Dark Foliage Green on one side and Light Foliage Green on the other. Blend well on your palette. Paint one-stroke leaves (see page 11) with this mix, allowing the colors to vary for more interest. Occasionally add a touch of Candlelight to the lighter side of the brush for more highlighting. On the larger leaves, add a center vein with a no. 1 Jackie Shaw liner and Medium Foliage Green.

2 paint the tulips

Base the center petal of the yellow tulips with Sunbright Yellow, using a no. 12 shader. Shade one side with Antique Gold. With the no. 1 Jackie Shaw liner and Sunbright Yellow + Antique Gold (1:1), paint three comma strokes on the shade side of the middle petal. Using the same brush and color, paint the linework on either side of the petal and the stamen lines. Overstroke the full length of the center petal opposite the three comma strokes with one stroke of White. Using the wood end of the liner, add stamen dots and stem dots of descending size.

3 paint the asters

Using a no. 20 shader double loaded with White into Purple Dusk and blended slightly on the palette, paint the purple asters with a chisel petal stroke (see page 11). Paint the calyx in three strokes with a no. 8 shader double loaded into Sunbright Yellow and Light Foliage Green, blended well on the palette.

4 paint the blue flowers

For the blue flowers, double load a no. 16 shader with White into Blue Jay, blending well on the palette. Use a petal stroke for each petal. (see page 11) The flower center is painted with Sunbright Yellow, using a no. 8 shader, and shaded with Antique Gold.

5 paint the daisies

Paint the daisy petals with White, using a no. 6 round stroke brush. Start at the outside end, press down and pull up to the brush tip at the flower center. Paint the center with Sunbright Yellow, using a no. 8 shader. Shade the center bottom with Antique Gold. Let dry. Then, with a fine-point permanent black ink pen, "stitch" around the center and crosshatch the inside of the center. Highlight the center with White checks painted with a no. 2 shader.

6 paint the roses

Base the roses with Indiana Rose, using a no. 12 shader. Use Wild Rose to shade the outside petals where they connect to the center section. Also shade the base and the hollow of the center section. With a side-load float of Peony, highlight the top edge of the center, the area below the hollow, and the outside edges of the outer petals.

7 paint the bell flowers

Base the purple bell flowers with Pale Lilac, using a no. 8 shader. Shade the bell base with Lilac and repeat with Deep Lilac. Add Lilac stamen lines, using a no. 1 Jackie Shaw liner. Top the flower with a wavy White line. With the brush tip, dot the stamen ends, some with Sunbright Yellow and some with White. Place a Sunbright Yellow dot at the flower base where it connects to the stem. (This dot appears in the next step.)

8 add checks, filler flowers and details

With the 1-inch (25mm) wash, paint two rows of White checks around the border, starting at the corners and working into the middle. Now add filler flowers to the empty areas. Paint the stems with Medium Foliage Green, using a no. 1 Jackie Shaw liner. Paint one-stroke leaves, using a no. 8 shader double loaded with Dark Foliage Green into Light Foliage Green blended well on the palette. With the wood end of a no. 1 Jackie Shaw liner, dot in four White petals and a Sunbright Yellow center. Use a fine-point permanent black ink pen to add stitching lines around the inside edge of the border, the flower details, the outlines, and the bows.

Mist the ink with Delta Ceramcoat Matte Interior Spray Varnish to prevent the ink from bleeding when the final varnish is applied. Allow the floorcloth to dry thoroughly. Erase any visible pattern lines with a brown gum eraser and then varnish (see page 13).

colorful kites

The use of primary colors is a popular decorating trend for children's rooms. Here's a simple way to bring those bright colors into a bedroom, playroom or even a porch. The many colors in the kites' tails just add to the fun. You can hardly look at this floorcloth without feeling your spirits rise.

colors
paint (Delta Ceramcoat)

blue mist	opaque yellow	blue bayou	opaque red
white	trail tan	spice brown	golden brown
ocean reef blue	opaque blue	fuchsia	black cherry
drizzle grey	pretty pink	lime sorbet	paradise
spring green	amethyst	passion	mediterranean	bahama purple

materials

surface
Fredrix floorcloth canvas, 2' x 3' (61cm x 91cm)

brushes (Loew-Cornell)
Shader, series 7300: nos. 4, 14 & 16 ~ Jackie Shaw liner, series JS: no. 2 ~ Script liner, series 7050: no. 1

additional supplies
2- to 4-inch (51mm to 102mm) sponge roller ~ ½-inch wide (13mm) Scotch Magic Tape ~ Pencil ~ Quilter's ruler ~ Tracing paper ~ Dark graphite paper and stylus ~ Small round sponge ~ Fine-point permanent black ink pen ~ Brown gum eraser ~ Delta Ceramcoat Matte Interior Spray Varnish ~ Delta Ceramcoat Satin Interior Varnish ~ Large flat or mop brush for final varnishing

(patterns for this floorcloth are on page 114)

1 base background and paint border

Basecoat the entire floorcloth with Blue Mist, using a sponge roller. Let dry. Place ½-inch (13mm) tape around the floorcloth edges. Place a second row of tape ¾" (19mm) from the floorcloth edge, leaving a ¼-inch (6mm) stripe. Seal the tape edges with basecoat to prevent bleeding (see page 12). Let dry and then repaint the stripe with Opaque Yellow. You may need two coats. Remove the tape. With a no. 14 shader, paint Blue Bayou checks along the outer mat edge, starting in the corners and working toward the center. Using a no. 1 script liner, paint an Opaque Red line ¼" (6mm) inside the yellow stripe. You can do this free-hand or draw a pencil guideline. Transfer randomly spaced kites onto the mat.

2 dab in clouds

Add White clouds with a small round sponge, dabbing in the fluffy cloud tops and softening out the bottoms with horizontal pulls of the sponge.

3 start the yellow kite(s)

Basecoat the yellow kite(s) with Opaque Yellow, using a no. 16 shader. Let dry. Then double load the brush with Opaque Yellow into White. Blend well on the palette. Highlight the outer kite edges, mostly on the left side. Using a no. 2 Jackie Shaw liner and Trail Tan, stroke in the kite sticks from point to point. With the same brush, shade with Spice Brown on all the stick ends and on both sides of the long stick where it intersects the short stick. Highlight the stick intersection with White.

4 add kite stick shadows

Using Golden Brown and a no. 16 shader, add shadows in the four corners where the sticks cross, letting the shadows continue and fade out along the length of the sticks. Shadows are strongest on the right side of the long stick.

5 paint the blue kite(s)

Paint the blue kite(s) in the same manner as the yellow (steps 3 and 4). Basecoat with Blue Bayou and highlight with Ocean Reef Blue. Stick colors do not change. Kite shadows are Opaque Blue.

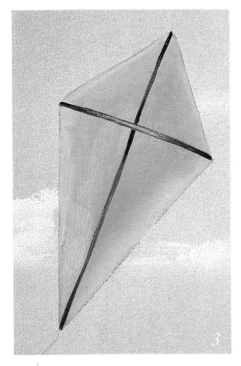

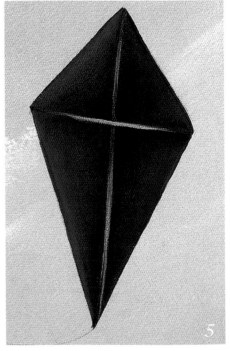

6 paint the red kite(s)

Paint the red kite(s) as you did the yellow and blue. Base with Opaque Red; highlight with Fuchsia; shade with Black Cherry. Stick colors do not change.

7 paint the kite tails

Paint the kite string with Drizzle Grey on a no. 1 script liner. Freehand kite tail bows, using bright palette colors (page 35) and a no. 4 shader. Add bow-fold details with a fine-point permanent black ink pen. Mist ink with Delta's Matte Interior Spray Varnish to prevent bleeding. Let dry thoroughly. Erase visible pattern lines with a brown gum eraser and then varnish (see page 13).

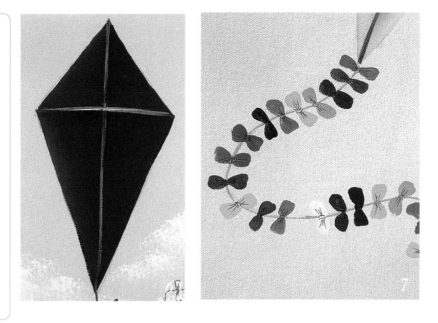

Carry out the colorful kite theme with a footstool (item #074 from Wayne's Woodenware). It not only provides a step up to high shelves but can be used as a low table for children sitting on the floor.

colonial village on sisal

Country-style enthusiasts, this easy-to-paint colonial house mat is for you! Simple and charming, it would look lovely on an enclosed porch or in front of your fireplace. Sisal mats are readily available and offer an interesting texture to paint on. Of course, any design painted on sisal would look equally great on canvas.

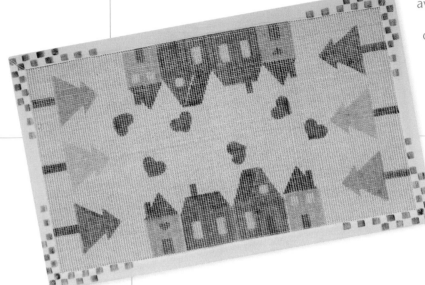

colors
paint (Delta Ceramcoat)

 rainforest green

charcoal

barn red

straw

 dark foliage green

cape cod blue

leaf green

burnt umber

materials
surface
Sisal mat with cotton twill binding,
27" x 45" (69cm x 114cm)

brushes (Loew-Cornell)
Wash, series 7150 or 7550: ¾-inch (19mm)

additional supplies
Masking tape ~ Plastic graph paper ~ Fine-point permanent ink pen ~ Scissors ~ Ruler or measuring tape ~ Round craft sponge ~ Delta Ceramcoat Matte Interior Spray Varnish ~

(stencil patterns for this mat are on page 116)

making your own stencil

You don't need to shop for stencils to paint this design—just make your own.

here's how

*1)*Enlarge the patterns to the appropriate percentage. *2)*Place a sheet of plastic graph paper over an enlarged pattern shape and trace the outline onto the plastic with a fine-point permanent ink pen. Windows, doors and hearts are shown on the house patterns for placement. You'll need to trace separate stencils for these shapes. *3)*If you trace more than one stencil shape on a sheet of plastic graph paper, leave at least 1½" (38mm) between shapes. *4)*Use scissors to pierce the middle of the plastic stencil shape. Cut out the shape, leaving a stencil hole. Repeat for all the shapes.

That's all there is to it.
You never need to give up on a design idea because you can't find the right stencil.

Instead, create it yourself!

1 start stenciling the first house

Apply masking tape to protect the cotton twill binding. Then use the project patterns to create stencils as explained above. Tape a narrow house stencil on one of the long sides of the mat so the left side of the house is about 12½" (32cm) from the left end of the mat. Then use tape to mask off the roof portion of the stencil. Load a round craft sponge with Rainforest Green and stencil in the bottom portion of the house. The paint will cover only the top "nubby" texture of the sisal rug. Let dry.

2 finish the first house

Remove the masking tape from the upper part of the house and then mask the lower part of the house. Stencil the roof and chimney with Charcoal. Carefully remove the masking and the house stencil. Let the roof and chimney dry. Then tape down the door stencil and sponge on Charcoal. Remove the stencil and let the door dry. Then tape the heart stencil above the door and sponge on Barn Red. Remove the stencil and let the heart dry.

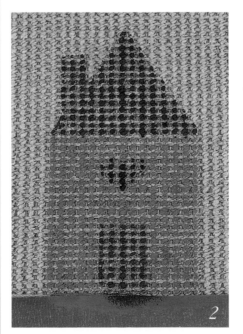

stenciling tip

Rinse the sponge every time you change stenciling paint to prevent muddying the colors. Working with several sponges can save time.

3 stencil the second house

Using the same technique as you did in steps 1 and 2, stencil the large house next to the first house. Use Barn Red for the lower portion, Charcoal for the roof and chimney and Straw for the windows.

4 stencil remaining houses and hearts

Next comes the house with front and side views. Secure and mask the stencil as you did for the previous houses. Sponge in Dark Foliage Green on the lower house portion and on the gable. Use Charcoal for the roof, Barn Red for the door and Straw for the windows. The second narrow house is stenciled with Cape Cod Blue on the bottom, Charcoal on the roof, Barn Red on the door and Straw on the windows. The hearts in the middle of the mat are stenciled with Barn Red.

5 stencil the trees

Now you're ready to stencil the trees on the short ends of the mat. Start with the middle tree, centering the tree stencil 23½" (60cm) from either edge. Use Leaf Green for the leafy portion of this middle tree. All the tree trunks are Burnt Umber. Use Rainforest Green for the leafy portion of the tree to the left and Dark Foliage Green for the leafy portion of the tree on the right.

design tip

Don't feel your "village" must look exactly like mine. You can place the houses in any order—just be sure to center your village on each side of the mat. You may choose to place the doors and windows differently. You can also switch house colors—although you'll want to avoid putting two houses of the same color next to each other. Have fun!

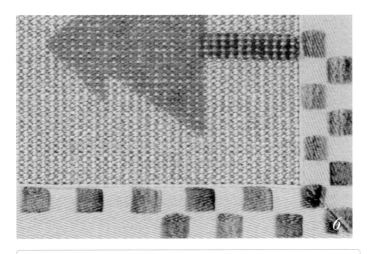

6 paint corner checks

Detail the sisal mat with a checkerboard design in the corners of the cotton twill binding. First remove the masking tape from the binding. Then load a ¾" (19mm) wash brush into thinned Dark Foliage Green and paint two rows of checkerboard squares starting in each corner and working your way out. Let the color fade as you go. Let all the paint dry completely. Protect the painted areas with a light misting of Delta Ceramcoat Matte Interior Spray Varnish.

sisal mat tip

This design would work equally well on canvas, but I love the texture of sisal. Check underneath the mat regularly and vacuum often to remove abrasive sand. With this simple care, your mat will last a very long time.

flowerpot garden

If impressionistic painting is your delight, then this design will be, too. Turn "dabs" of color into beautiful pots of flowers! The texture of the sisal weave only adds to the effect. Create a charming vignette by placing the mat near one or more accent flowerpots painted with similar impressionistic flowers.

colors
paint *(Delta Ceramcoat)*

desert sun orange	burnt sienna	island coral	blue spruce
wild rose	hydrangea pink	sunbright yellow	village green
mediterranean	blue mist	leaf green	amethyst
pale lilac	dark foliage green	white	burnt umber

materials
surface
Sisal mat with cotton twill binding,
20" x 36" (51cm x 91cm)

brushes *(Loew-Cornell)*
Wash, series 7150 or 7550: ¾-inch (19mm)
~ Script liner, series 7050: no. 4

additional supplies
Plastic graph paper ~ Fine-point permanent
black ink pen ~ Pencil ~ Scissors ~ Masking tape ~
Ruler or measuring tape ~ Round craft sponge ~
Delta Ceramcoat Matte Interior Spray Varnish

(pattern for this mat is on page 115)

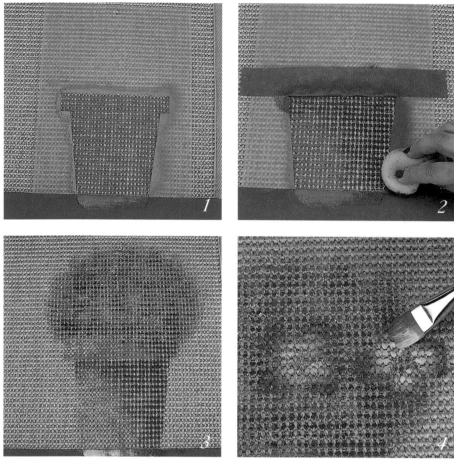

1 stencil first flowerpot

Create a flowerpot stencil (see page 39, "Making Your Own Stencil"). Use masking tape to protect the cotton twill binding on one of the long sides of the mat. Place the flowerpot stencil above the tape. Position the right pot rim edge about 4½" (11cm) from the mat's right edge. Load a round craft sponge into Desert Sun Orange and stencil the color onto the nubby texture of the sisal. Let dry.

2 shade the flowerpot

Press a line of masking tape over the rim of the clay pot. Shade the right side of the clay pot by loading a clean edge of the round craft sponge into Burnt Sienna and stenciling under the pot rim and down the right side. Let dry. Remove the tape from the rim and shade the right side of the rim with a soft stipple of sponged Burnt Sienna.

3 highlight pot and base foliage

Using a clean edge of the sponge, highlight the left side of the pot rim and down the left side of the pot body with a soft stipple of Island Coral. Paint a mound of background foliage color by sponging on Blue Spruce with a clean sponge. Let the color fade around the mound edges.

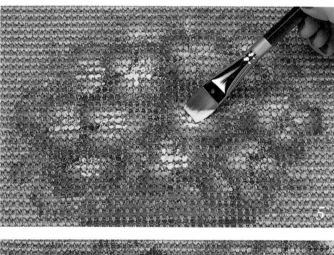

4 stroke in rose flowers

Heavily double load a ¾" (19mm) wash with Wild Rose and Hydrangea Pink. Paint four C-stroke petals to form each full flower, keeping the lighter color toward the flower center. C-stroke petals are petal strokes (page 11) with a curve. The heavy brush loading lets the flowers show up well on the sisal.

5 edge with partial flowers

Paint partial flower blossoms around the outside edge of the background mound of foliage color. Let some of the flower petals extend over the pot rim These partial blossoms should fade away from the outside edges. Load Sunbright Yellow on the ¾" (19mm) wash and dab flower centers into the middle of the full flowers.

6 finish pots and paint blue flowers

Stencil the remaining pots as explained in steps 1 through 3. Leave about 1½" (4cm) between rim edges. Sponge in Village Green for background foliage of the blue flowers. Double load the ¾" (19mm) wash with Mediterranean and Blue Mist and paint C-stroke petals. Keep the lighter blue side of the brush towards the flower centers. Dab in the flower centers with Sunbright Yellow loaded on a ¾" (19mm) wash.

7 paint purple and yellow flowers

Now paint the purple flowers, following the same technique as you did for the rose and blue flowers. Use Leaf Green for the background foliage. Paint the C-stroke flowers with double-loaded Amethyst and Pale Lilac, keeping the lighter side of the brush toward the flower centers. Paint the centers Sunbright Yellow.

For the yellow flowers, sponge the background foliage in Dark Foliage Green. Paint the yellow flowers with Sunbright Yellow side loaded onto a ¾" (19mm) wash. Then paint the flower centers White.

8 add corner vines

Finish the sisal mat with a corner vining design. Paint the vining with a no. 4 script liner and thinned Burnt Umber. Paint the leaves with a ¾" (19mm) wash double loaded into Blue Spruce and Village Green. Use lots of paint on the brush and paint one-stroke leaves (see page 11) here and there along the vining. Begin in the corners, letting the color fade and the leaf size diminish as the vine continues. Let all the paint dry completely. Protect the painted areas with a light misting of Delta Ceramcoat Matte Interior Spray Varnish.

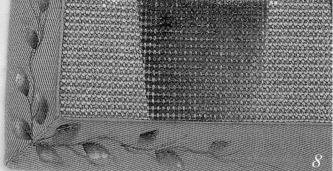

This flowerpot design seems to cry out for an actual coordinating clay flowerpot.

black and white toile

Toile is everywhere—on fabrics, wallpapers, table accessories and clothing. Complete your decorating look with a toile floorcloth. If black and white isn't to your taste, try one of the color suggestions mentioned in the color tip below. Although this design looks complicated, a quick read through the instructions will convince you otherwise.

colors
paint *(Delta Ceramcoat)*

light ivory   charcoal

color tip

Try different toile color schemes. Just match a wallpaper, gift wrap or fabric swatch to Delta paints. Sheer the paint with a little water to test the color. Moroccan Red works well for red designs, Blue Storm and Cape Cod for blue and Burnt Umber for brown.

moroccan red   blue storm   cape cod   burnt umber

materials
surface
Fredrix floorcloth canvas, 2' x 3' (61cm x 91cm)

brushes *(Loew-Cornell)*
Wash, series 7150 or 7550: ¾-inch (19mm), 1-inch (25mm) ~ Shader, series 7300: nos. 4 & 16 ~ Mop, series 275: 1-inch (25mm) ~ Script liner, series 7050: no. 4

additional supplies
2- to 4-inch (51mm to 102mm) sponge roller ~ Pencil ~ Quilter's ruler ~ Fine-point permanent black ink pen ~ Tracing paper ~ Gray graphite paper and stylus ~ Masking tape ~ Brown gum eraser ~ Delta Ceramcoat Satin Interior Varnish ~ Large flat or mop brush for varnishing

(patterns for the floorcloth are on page 117)

1 basecoat floorcloth and mark diamonds

Basecoat the floorcloth in Light Ivory with a sponge roller. Let dry. Using a regular pencil and a quilter's ruler, measure and mark off a border area where the diamond shapes will be applied. Make this border 6" (15cm) wide along the long sides of the floor-cloth and 4" (10cm) wide along the short sides. Measure and mark off all the diamond shapes, using the diamond pattern on page 117 and the quilter's ruler. The top and bottom points of the diamonds touch the outside edge of the floorcloth and the inside border line. Once all the diamond shapes are spaced correctly and evenly, you can use the quilter's ruler and the fine-point permanent black ink pen to re-mark the diamond lines. Transfer the detailed flower patterns into the center field area.

2 trace over graphite lines with ink

Using the fine-point permanent black ink pen, trace over the graphite lines of the center field floral pattern. Also trace over the border line separating the floral field from the border area. Use a quilter's ruler to keep the lines straight.

3 shade the roses

Dampen a no. 16 shader with water and side load into a scant amount of Charcoal. Blend well on a waxed palette. Start in the middle of the rose and work out. Shade the base of each petal with a side-load float of sheer Charcoal, keeping the darker side of the brush toward the center of the flower on most petals.

pen tip

You'll find permanent ink pens in hobby and craft stores. They come in a variety of point widths. Experiment! Use a broader point for outlining and a small point for details.

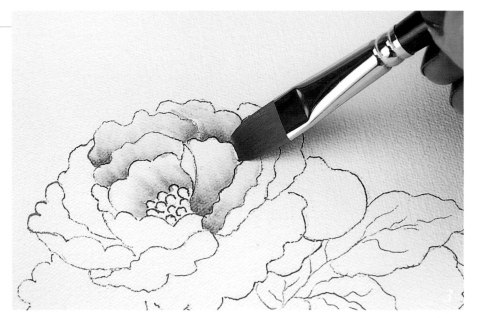

4 shade leaves and smaller flowers

Continue shading all design areas, switching to a ¾-inch (19mm) wash for the leaves and larger design elements. Shade each leaf at the base and partially along the lower edge. Shade the five-petal flowers using the no. 16 shader, keeping the darker side of the brush toward the center of the flower.

5 deepen shading

Add dimension to the floral design by deepening the shading on some flower petals and leaves with an additional side-load float of Charcoal. Paint the small dark filler leaves with a no. 4 shader and Charcoal that has been thinned with a small amount of water.

6 paint the diamonds

Mix a puddle of Charcoal thinned with water. Load a 1-inch (25mm) wash with the thinned Charcoal and basecoat the diamonds on the border area.

shading tip

Moistening the area you wish to shade with a scant amount of clear water gives you more time to apply and work out your shading color. For perfect results, apply the shading color with a large side-loaded flat or shader. Pit-pat the color into the shade area and then softly stipple over the same area with a dry mop brush. The mop stipple softens brush marks into the surface without moving the paint color out of the shade area. Let dry and repeat once or twice to achieve the proper width and color depth.

7 shade corners and detail the edge

Shading the field corners helps set this area back into the border. First mask the corners of the border area. Then dampen the corners of the field area with clear water. Load a dampened 1-inch (25mm) wash into very sheer Charcoal and float shading into the field corners, softening out into the field area with gently applied 1-inch (25mm) mop brush stippling. Remove the masking tape immediately and clean up any paint that has bled underneath with the edge of a clean brush. Finish the floorcloth by detailing the outside edge with a line of thinned Charcoal painted with a no. 4 script liner (see below). Allow the floorcloth to dry completely. Erase any visible pattern lines with a brown gum eraser and then varnish (see page 13).

7

french country

Here's a floorcloth for French country décor lovers. This design is a real eye-catcher—and don't the bright and cheerful colors make you want to smile? What a great addition to a French country kitchen—or any other room in your home.

colors
paint *(Delta Ceramcoat)*

crocus yellow	mello yellow	liberty blue	light ivory
moroccan red	pine green	leprechaun	white
	crocus yellow + mello yellow (2:1)	moroccan red + light ivory (1:1)	

materials
surface
Fredrix floorcloth canvas, 2' x 3' (61cm x 91cm)

brushes *(Loew-Cornell)*
Wash, series 7150 or 7550: ½-inch (13cm) ~
Shader, series 7300: nos. 2, 4, 6, 8, 10, 12, 16 & 20
~ Jackie Shaw liner, series JS: no. 1 ~
Script liner, series 7050: nos. 10/0, 1 & 2

additional supplies
Pencil ~ Quilter's ruler ~ 2- to 4-inch (51mm
to 102mm) sponge roller ~ Masking tape ~ Soapstone
pencil ~ Tracing paper ~ Dark graphite paper and
stylus ~ Brown gum eraser ~ Delta Ceramcoat Satin
Interior Varnish ~ Large flat or mop brush for varnishing

(patterns for this floorcloth are on page 118)

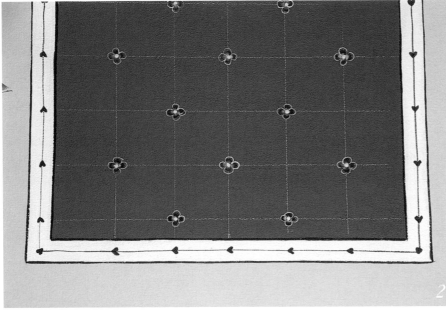

1 base, draw guidelines, transfer the pattern

With a pencil and quilter's ruler, measure and mark off two lines around the floor cloth, 6" (15cm) and 6¾" (17cm) from the edges. With a sponge roller, basecoat the outer border with Crocus Yellow + Mello Yellow (2:1) and the center panel with Liberty Blue, masking with tape as necessary to achieve straight lines. Basecoat the ¾-inch (19mm) stripe with Light Ivory using a ½-inch (13mm) wash.

Using a quilter's ruler and soapstone pencil, draw horizontal and vertical guidelines through the middle of the center section. Add guidelines on both sides of these first two lines, spacing them 1½" (4cm) apart. Transfer the flower patterns onto the outside border. You will use the flowers or elements of the flowers more than once. The order and placement are not important, but try to alternate between blue and red flowers.

2 detail panel and stripe

Double load a no. 2 shader with Light Ivory into Moroccan Red and paint the small, four-petal flowers on alternating intersections of the center panel guidelines. Add a center dot of Crocus Yellow + Mello Yellow (2:1) with the wood end of a no. 10/0 script liner. With the same brush and yellow mix, paint a thin outline around each flower.

Still using the no. 10/0 script liner, paint a Liberty Blue line down the center of the Light Ivory stripe. Using the soapstone lines in the center panel as placement guides, paint small Moroccan Red hearts with a no. 1 Jackie Shaw liner on the blue line. Outline both sides of the Light Ivory stripe with Moroccan Red, using a no. 1 script liner.

tracing tip

When you trace this pattern, do it in small sections of individual flowers. This gives you the freedom to rearrange the placement of the flowers as you go around the floorcloth border. If you repeat the pattern exactly as given, it could look stiff. Just try to alternate the flowers and berries so you don't have design elements of the same color next to each other

3 paint stems and leaves

All the stems are painted with Pine Green, using a no. 1 script liner. One flower formation should flow into the next flower formation. Paint the leaves with a double load of Leprechaun into Crocus Yellow, using a variety of shaders, such as nos. 8, 12 and 16, to get different sizes of leaves. All leaves are one-stroke leaves (see page 11). Returning to Pine Green and a no. 1 script liner, add veins and loosely outline some of the leaves. In any open area, you may add a tendril to fill and expand the flowers.

4 paint the blue daisies

a) Paint the blue daisy petals with a no. 20 shader double loaded with White into Liberty Blue. Use chisel petal strokes (see page 11).
b) Paint the centers with Crocus Yellow, using a no. 6 shader. Highlight the top of the center with White.
c) With the no. 1 Jackie Shaw liner, paint three Liberty Blue strokes, going over the White highlight into the center. With a stylus, add Liberty Blue dots around the bottom of the center. Finish with a White stroke at the base of the blue stroke, using a no. 1 Jackie Shaw liner.

5 paint the berries

Basecoat the berries with Moroccan Red, using a no. 4 shader. Highlight with Moroccan Red + Light Ivory (1:1). With Pine Green, give each berry a stem and a few strokes on the blossom end, using a no. 1 Jackie Shaw liner.

6 paint the roses

Paint the roses with a double load of Moroccan Red + Light Ivory (1:1) into Light Ivory, using a no. 10 shader. Each rose is a cluster of comma strokes (see page 10) with the red mix to the outside of each stroke. With Leprechaun and a no. 4 shader, add two or three one-stroke calyx leaves at the base of each rose.

7 paint the bluebells

a) Begin painting the bluebells with a double load of Light Ivory into Liberty Blue, using a no. 6 shader. The flowers consist of two comma strokes, one to the left and one to the right. Keep the Liberty Blue to the outside of the flower. b) Overstroke one petal of each flower with White, using a no. 1 Jackie Shaw liner. c) With the same brush, add three Liberty Blue strokes coming from the center of the flower.

8 paint the four-petal flowers

a) Paint the blue four-petal flowers with a no. 10 shader double loaded with Liberty Blue into Light Ivory. Use the petal stroke (see page 11). b) With a stylus, loosely fill the centers with Crocus Yellow dots. c) Add Leprechaun dots in the open spaces between the yellow dots. Paint the bud calyxes with two one-stroke leaves, using a no. 4 shader and Leprechaun.

9 paint the five-petal flowers

a) Paint the red five-petal flowers, using a no. 8 shader and Moroccan Red + Light Ivory (1:1). Each petal is painted as a large C-stroke (see tip on this page), keeping the red to the outside. b) Loosely outline the petals with Moroccan Red, using a no. 10/0 script liner. c) Paint the centers with a no. 4 shader, double loaded with Liberty Blue into White. Add center dots with a stylus and Liberty Blue.

c-stroke tip

To paint C-stroke flower petals, stand the brush on the chisel edge, press down in a curved motion and return to the chisel for the other side of the petal.

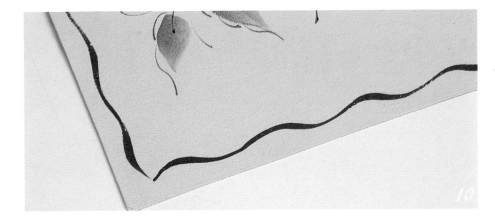

lifeline tip

When painting a lifeline,
use a script liner loaded with paint
thinned with water to ink-like consistency.
To create a nice, consistent look, raise the
brush more to the tip as you are pulling to
the right and apply a small amount of
pressure as you are pulling to the left.
The result should look like a
continuous S-stroke.

10 add the lifeline edging

Using a no. 2 script liner, paint a Moroccan Red wavy lifeline ½" (13mm) from the mat edge. Allow the floorcloth to dry thoroughly. Erase any visible pattern or marking lines with a brown gum eraser and then varnish (see page 13).

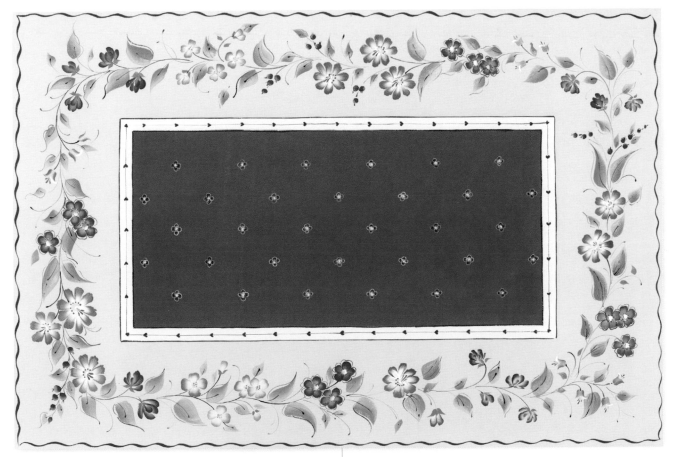

So many people commented on how much they like this French country design, I felt it deserved an extra special accessory like this chest (item #PC115 from Wood Concepts).

blue strokes

Blue-and-white décor is very popular today. This design is elegant in a simple way, and it could easily be adapted to many other color themes. Have fun creating the right combination of colors for your home. The scrolls and strokework in the center are painted freehand with the help of guidelines. If you're unaccustomed to this type of work, a little practice will give you confidence.

materials

surface

Fredrix floorcloth canvas, 2' x 3' (61cm x 91cm)

brushes (Loew-Cornell)

Wash, series 7150 or 7550: ½-inch (13mm) ~
Shader, series 7300: nos. 8 & 14 ~ Deerfoot stippler,
series 7850: ¼-inch (6mm) ~ Jackie Shaw liner,
series JS: no. 2 ~ Script liner, series 7050: no. 1

additional supplies

2- to 4-inch (51mm to 102mm) sponge roller ~ Pencil ~
Quilter's ruler ~ Tracing paper ~ Dark transfer paper
and stylus ~ Brown gum eraser ~ Delta Ceramcoat Satin
Interior Varnish ~ Large flat or mop brush for varnishing

(the patterns for this floorcloth are on page 119)

colors
paint (Delta Ceramcoat)

| light ivory | tide pool blue | cape cod blue |
| white | light ivory + tide pool blue (2:1)white | |

1 base and transfer patterns

Basecoat the entire cloth with Light Ivory, using a sponge roller. With a pencil and quilter's ruler, mark off two lines, one 5½" (14cm) and another 6" (15cm), creating a ½" (13mm) stripe inside a 5½" (14cm) border. Using the photo on the opposite page as a guide for placement, transfer the border patterns with dark graphite paper and a stylus.

2 draw panel guidelines and paint stripe

Use a quilter's ruler and pencil to draw a line from one corner of the inner panel to the diagonal corner. Add diagonal lines at 3" (8cm) intervals on either side of the corner-to-corner diagonal. Starting with the other two panel corners, follow the same procedure to draw a second series of diagonals across the first, creating a diamond pattern. These are your guidelines for the inner panel scrolls and strokework.

Now paint the ½" (13mm) stripe with Light Ivory + Tide Pool Blue (2:1) on a ½-inch (13mm) wash.

3 paint scrolls and strokework

Paint the scroll-and-stroke pattern in the center panel with Tide Pool Blue. Use a no. 1 script liner for the scrolls and a no. 2 Jackie Shaw liner for the strokes.

scroll & stroke tip

Smaller scrolls can be painted with a liner, as described in step 3. For larger scrolls, use a side-loaded brush. This creates a soft look with color along the scroll edge flowing to no color on the inside of the scroll. Then outline the scroll with a fine liner to give it definition.

4 paint border flowers

Paint the flowers with a side-load float of Tide Pool Blue, using a no. 14 shader and the petal stroke (see page 11). Using the same side-load float, paint one side of the leaves.

5 add s-strokes and comma strokes

Paint the border S-strokes and comma strokes (see page 10) with a side-load float of Tide Pool Blue, using a no. 8 shader.

6 paint floral details

Paint the detail linework that outlines the flowers and leaves with the no. 1 script liner and Cape Cod Blue. Using the same color on a no. 2 Jackie Shaw liner, add three strokes in each flower petal, a center vein in each large leaf, and a stroke on each side of the half-flower. Using the wood end of the no. 2 Jackie Shaw liner, apply three dots of Cape Cod Blue at the four corners of the border (see finished mat on opposite page for placement) and at the ends of the stems of the half-flowers.

7 stipple and dot flower centers

Using the ¼-inch (6mm) deerfoot, stipple in the flower centers with Light Ivory + Tide Pool Blue (2:1). Tip the toe of the brush into Tide Pool Blue and stipple shading on one side of the centers. Still using the deerfoot, highlight the other side of the center with White. Using a stylus, dot around the outside edge of the flower centers with White.

blending tip

To give your flowers a soft look, remember to blend the side-loaded brush several times on the palette before stroking on a petal. Using a larger brush gives you room to blend from color to no color. Also remember to blend both sides of the brush.

8 touch up stripe and paint corner details

Using Tide Pool Blue on the no. 1 script liner, clean up the edges of the ½" (13mm) stripe and also draw a thin outer corner stripe about ½" (13mm) from the edge of the floorcloth. For the corner stripes, start at the point of the corners and allow the stripe to fade as you pull away. Allow the floor cloth to dry thoroughly. Erase all visible pattern lines with a brown gum eraser and then varnish (see page 13).

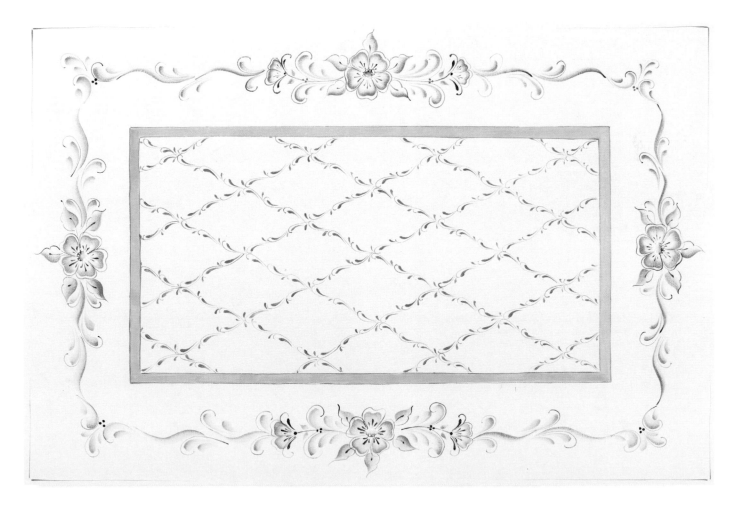

tone on tone strokes

This floorcloth was painted in trendy soft sage greens, but this design could be easily done in any color combination. Pick a light background color for the inner panel and a contrasting color of your choice. Mix the two for the border background and for the strokework in the center. Use the lighter background color for the border design. Have fun creating your own look!

materials

surface
Fredrix floorcloth canvas, 2' x 3' (61cm x 91cm)

brushes (Loew-Cornell)
Round stroke, series 7040: no. 8 ~
Script liner, series 7050: no. 2

additional supplies
2- to 4-inch (51mm to 102mm)
sponge roller ~ Pencil ~Quilter's ruler ~
Brown gum eraser ~ Delta Ceramcoat
Satin Interior Varnish ~ Large flat or
mop brush for varnishing

(the pattern for this floorcloth is on page 119)

colors
paint (Delta Ceramcoat)

| antique white | silver pine | silver pine + antique white (1:1) |

scroll and stroke tip

The center portion of this floorcloth is painted freehand. If you're not accustomed to freehand scrolling and strokework, a little practice before you begin the floorcloth will give you the confidence you need to go ahead.

1 base and draw painting guidelines

Basecoat the entire cloth with Antique White, using a sponge roller. Let dry. With a pencil and quilter's ruler, mark off a 5" (13cm) border and basecoat the border with Silver Pine + Antique White (1:1).

To make the border scrollwork come out even on all sides, you will now section off the sides. Start by drawing a diagonal line from the corner of the inner panel to the corner of the cloth. Measure and mark the halfway point of the short ends. Then divide and mark each of these sections in half again. This should create four equal sections on both ends, each section about 4½" (11cm) long. For the long sides, measure and mark the halfway mark and then divide each half section into thirds, creating six sections per side, each section about 5" (13cm) long. Transfer the border motif pattern into each of the marked sections—or, if you prefer, you may paint the border freehand.

2 paint border scrolls and strokework

All border scrolls and strokework are painted in Antique White. *a)* With a no. 2 script liner, paint the thin scroll lines, each extending the length of a section. *b)* The rest of the border design is painted with a no. 8 round stroke brush. Paint two long comma strokes (see page 10) inside the curve of the long scroll lines. *c)* Close off the space on the left with two more long comma strokes. *d)* To the right of the scroll, paint an S-stroke (see page 10). Then paint a large dot at the base of each group of strokes.

3 detail the corners

With the no. 2 script liner, pull lines from the point of the corners, letting the lines fade out. Add a dot to the corner point. Paint this corner treatment on both the inside and outside border corners. With the no. 8 round stroke brush, add three comma strokes to the corner strokework groups.

4 freehand center strokework

The scrolls and strokework in the center panel are all done in Silver Pine + Antique White (1:1). With the no. 2 script liner, paint long scrollwork lines freehand, beginning each new line on the curve of a previous line.

5 add long comma strokes

With the no. 8 round stroke, fill in the inner curve of the scrollwork strokes with long comma strokes. Follow the curve of the scrollwork.

6 paint filler strokes

Using the same brush, fill in the empty spaces with additional long comma strokes. Each stroke should follow the curve of a thin scrollwork line. There's no specific placement for these strokes—go for a pattern that pleases the eye. When the center panel is filled, allow the floorcloth to dry thoroughly, erase visible pencil lines with a brown gum eraser and then varnish (see page 13).

This scroll-and-strokework design has an elegance that makes it perfect for a serving plate (item #P1410 from Wayne's Woodenware). When not in use, the piece can be displayed for its sheer loveliness.

seasonal floorcloths

This seasonal section includes designs suitable for many favorite holidays and every season of the year! Enjoy the bold pinks of "Heart of the Home." Welcome spring as well as your guests with "Garden Welcome." Celebrate Easter with the dreamy pastels of "Easter Eggs." Our "Spooky Night" Halloween floorcloth won't scare the neighborhood children, but it will delight them. "Autumn Leaves" casually brings the outdoors inside. Many of these designs are child-friendly. For example, "Stars and Stripes" is an easy sponging project and "Midnight Snowfall" is painted with simple-to-use stencils. Whatever your favorite time of year, celebrate it with painting.

heart of the home

Quick and easy to paint, this heart sampler floorcloth will surely let someone know how much you really love him or her—not only on Valentine's Day but all year long. The diagram on page 66 enables you to achieve the exact position, pattern and color combinations I used, but feel free to experiment.

materials

surface

Fredrix floorcloth canvas, 2' x 3' (61cm x 91cm)

brushes (Loew-Cornell)

Wash, series 7150 or 7550: ½-inch (13mm) ~ Shader, series 7300, no. 8 ~ Deerfoot stippler, series 7850: ½-inch (13mm) ~ Script liner, series 7050: no. 4

additional supplies

2- to 4-inch (51mm to 102mm) sponge roller ~ Pencil ~ Quilter's ruler ~ Tracing paper ~ Dark graphite paper and stylus ~ Funky Patterns stencil, #BLM-508 from American Traditional Stencils ~ A few paper towels ~ Brown gum eraser ~ Delta Ceramcoat Satin Interior Varnish ~ Large flat or mop brush for varnishing

(patterns for this floorcloth are on page 119)

colors

paint *(Delta Ceramcoat)*

light ivory · pink parfait · berry red · hydrangea pink

fuchsia · fiesta pink

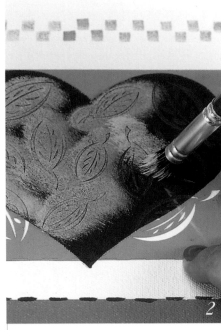

1 basecoat, mark and transfer

Basecoat the entire floorcloth with Light Ivory and a sponge roller. Using a quilter's ruler and a pencil, measure and mark a 3" (8cm) border around the floorcloth. Basecoat the border with Pink Parfait.

In the Light Ivory field, measure and mark off 6" x 6" (15cm x 15cm) squares. Using thinned Pink Parfait and a no. 8 shader, paint two rows of checker trim, one row each on either side of the square outlines. Let dry. Using a no. 4 script liner, outline the Light Ivory field with a stitching line of thinned Berry Red. Let dry.

Transfer the large heart-shaped pattern into the center of all squares. Using a ½-inch (13mm) wash, basecoat each heart in its appropriate color (refer to the schematic and key on this page). As you work through subsequent steps you may also use this schematic to help you with the placement and color of the decorative patterns within the hearts.

2 stencil leaf pattern

Place the leaf stencil over a Berry Red heart. Load the ½-inch (13mm) deerfoot stippler into Hydrangea Pink, pounce off the extra paint onto a paper towel and then stencil the leaf design onto the heart.

making the heart schematic

As you work through this project, you can use this schematic to help you with the placement and color of the decorative patterns within the hearts.

1	2	3	1	4
2	4	1	5	2
5	3	4	3	5

key

1
Fiesta Pink heart with Hydrangea Pink roses

2
Pink Parfait heart with Berry Red polka dots

3
Hydrangea Pink heart with Berry Red stars and spirals

4
Fuchsia heart with Hydrangea Pink stripes

5
Berry Red heart with Hydrangea Pink leaves

3 fill empty areas

Check the heart for blank areas, such as you see near the point of the heart in this photo. Reposition the stencil as needed and fill in these areas with additional leaf motifs, using the same color and brush.

4 add stitching lines

Here you can see how adding a portion of the leaf design to the point of the heart gives a more complete look. Finish the heart with a "stitched" outline of Berry Red, using a no. 4 script liner. Repeat steps 2, 3 and 4 for the remaining Berry Red hearts.

5 paint brush-handle dots

In the Pink Parfait hearts, randomly place Berry Red dots, using the handle end of any brush. Finish the hearts with stitched outlines of Pink Parfait, using a no. 4 script liner (outline not seen in this photo).

stencil tip

Avoid under-the-stencil paint bleeds by using a lighter paint load. If the paint does bleed, remove it immediately with a clean, damp paint brush.

6 stencil stripes

Apply the stripe stencil on a Fuchsia heart, using Hydrangea Pink and the ½-inch (13mm) deerfoot stippler. If the stencil doesn't cover the heart, move it, lining it up on one of the already stenciled stripes, and continue the stenciling. Finish the heart with a stitched outline of Fuchsia, using a no. 4 script liner. (Stitched outline not shown in this photo.) Repeat this step for the remaining Fuchsia hearts.

7 stencil roses

Place the rose stencil on top of a Fiesta Pink heart and apply the design with Hydrangea Pink, using the ½-inch (13mm) deerfoot stippler. Finish the heart with a stitched outline of Fiesta Pink, using a no. 4 script liner. Repaint this step for the remaining Fiesta Pink hearts.

8 stencil stars and spirals

Place the stars-and-spirals stencil on top of a Hydrangea Pink heart and apply the design with Berry Red, using the ½-inch (13mm) deerfoot stippler. Finish the heart with a stitched outline of Hydrangea Pink, using a no. 4 script liner. Repeat this step for the remaining Hydrangea Pink hearts.

design tip

You can create a pleasing random effect in the border by varying the number in the comma-stroke groupings. Make some two strokes, others three, avoiding a predictable pattern.

9 paint the border lifeline, stems and strokes

Use a no. 4 script liner to paint a wavy lifeline of Hydrangea Pink through the middle of the border area. Curl the lines together in the corners. Add short "stems" to each dip in the lifeline, using the same brush and color. Thin Hydrangea Pink with a little water and, with a no. 8 shader, paint comma stroke accents (see page 10) in groups of two or three along the lifeline.

10 stencil detail hearts in the border

Detail the ends of the border stem lines with small stenciled hearts of Berry Red. When dry, use the handle end of any brush to dot the pointed end of each heart with Light Ivory. Erase all visible pattern lines with a brown gum eraser and then varnish (see page 13).

garden welcome

This floorcloth is the perfect greeting for your guests. My inspiration was a plaque I designed for a class project (see page 75). Paint the floorcloth to place inside your front door or on a protected porch entrance. It's easy—just take it letter by letter and you'll be finished in no time.

colors
paint *(Delta Ceramcoat)*

moss green	black green	dark forest green	burnt umber	trail tan
white	burnt sienna	sunbright yellow	blue spruce	pretty pink
black cherry	spice brown	quaker grey	dark burnt umber	charcoal
flesh tan	light ivory	blue velvet	paradise	amethyst
bahama purple	caribbean blue	desert sun orange	sea grass	blue velvet + white (1:1)

materials

surface
Fredrix floorcloth canvas, 2' x 3' (61cm x 91cm), cut to 1½' x 3' (46cm x 91cm)

brushes *(Loew-Cornell)*
Wash, series 7150 or 7550: ¾-inch (19mm), 1-inch (25mm) ~ Shader, series 7300: nos. 4, 8, 10 ~ Deerfoot stippler, series 7850: ½-inch (13mm) ~ Mop, series 275: 1-inch (25mm) ~ Jackie Shaw liner, series JS: no. 1 ~ Script liner, series 7050: no. 4

additional supplies
2- to 4-inch (51mm to 102mm) sponge roller ~ Quilter's ruler ~ Pencil ~ Tracing paper ~ White graphite paper and stylus ~ Masking tape ~ Round craft sponge ~ Brown gum eraser ~ Delta Ceramcoat Satin Interior Varnish ~ Large flat or mop brush for varnishing

(the pattern for this floorcloth is on pages 120 & 121)

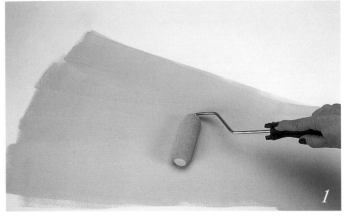

1 prepare floorcloth for design painting

Cut a pre-primed canvas floorcloth to 1½' x 3' (46cm x 91cm). Basecoat with Moss Green and a small sponge roller. Two coats may be needed to achieve opaque coverage. Let dry. With a quilter's ruler and pencil, measure and mark off a 3" (8cm) border around the entire floorcloth. Transfer the letter patterns onto the center field, using white graphite paper and a stylus.

2 shade the letters

Shade to the left and below each letter with a very soft side-load float of Black Green on a 1-inch (25mm) wash. To keep the shading soft, dampen the area to be shaded before applying the shade color. Soften the paint into the surface with a gentle stipple, using a dry 1-inch (25mm) mop.

3 paint vines

Paint thin stem lines along the "W," using thinned Dark Forest Green and a no. 4 script liner. Double load a no. 4 shader into Dark Forest Green and Moss Green. Then paint little one-stroke leaves (see page 11) along the stem lines.

Move on to the "E." Paint the vining along this letter in two layers, using a no. 1 Jackie Shaw liner for both. The first layer is thinned Burnt Umber; the second layer is Trail Tan.

4 add daisies, leaves and berries

Paint the mini-daisies on the "W" with the chisel edge of a no. 4 shader and White. Dab in the centers with a no. 4 shader double loaded into Burnt Sienna and Sunbright Yellow.

Paint one-stroke leaves along the vining of the "E," using a no. 8 shader and thinned Blue Spruce. The berries are painted with a no. 4 shader double loaded into Pretty Pink and Black Cherry. Add a highlight dot to the Pretty Pink side of each berry, using a no. 1 Jackie Shaw liner and White.

5 base, shade the shovel

The "L" is a garden shovel stuck into the ground. Base the shovel handle with a wash of Spice Brown on a no. 8 shader. Base the trowel with Quaker Grey. With a no. 1 Jackie Shaw liner, paint wood grain lines along the handle with thinned Dark Burnt Umber. Shade the area where the handle meets the trowel with a side-load float of Dark Burnt Umber on a no. 8 shader. Shade the left side and the indentation on the trowel with a side-load float of Charcoal.

6 highlight trowel and paint ground

Highlight the other side of the trowel with a side-load float of brush-mixed Quaker Grey + a touch of White. Highlight the handle of the shovel with a side-load float of Flesh Tan. Paint the ground area with a side-load float of Burnt Umber on a ¾-inch (19mm) wash, letting it fade out at the lower edge.

7 begin "C" and "O," paint eggs

Begin the "C" with stem lines of thinned Dark Forest Green painted with a no. 4 script liner. Paint the long thin leaves with a double load of Dark Forest Green and Light Ivory on a no. 4 shader.

Begin the "O" with a nest of vining painted with thinned Dark Burnt Umber on a no. 4 script liner. Widen the nest with additional lines around the "O" until it is about ¾" (19mm) wide and looks substantial enough to support bird eggs. Base the eggs with Blue Spruce and a no. 8 shader. Shade the egg bottoms with a side-load float of Blue Velvet. Highlight the top curves with a side-load float of Paradise.

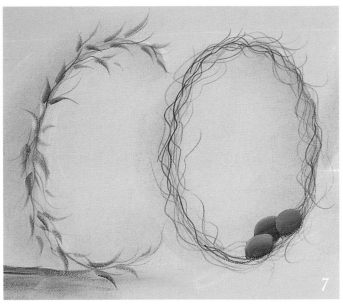

8 paint blossoms and complete vining and eggs

Paint the lavender blossoms on the "C" as very small C-strokes, using a no. 4 shader double loaded into Amethyst and Bahama Purple. C-strokes are like petal strokes (see page 11) with a curve.

Enhance the vining on the nest with additional thin vining layers of Spice Brown, Flesh Tan and a few rounds of White, painted with a no. 4 script liner. Tuck the eggs into the nest by trailing the layers of vining across the lower edge of the eggs. Highlight the top curves of the two foreground eggs with a side-load float of brush-mixed Caribbean Blue + a touch of White, using a no. 8 shader.

9 begin the "M" and the "E"

The letter "M" is composed of two topiaries in clay pots. Base the clay pots with Desert Sun Orange. Dampen the tree shapes with clean water and then stipple the shapes with Dark Forest Green, using a ½-inch (13mm) deerfoot stippler. Base the trunks with a line of Burnt Umber.

The letter "E" is an antique wooden rake. Base in the rake with thinned Spice Brown on a no. 10 shader.

10 complete the "M" and "E," paint the birds

While the trees are still damp, highlight with a soft stipple of Sea Grass followed by a little Moss Green on the right side of each tree for texture.

Detail the rake and handle with wood grain lines of thinned Dark Burnt Umber on a no. 4 script liner. Shade the rake and handle with a side-load float of Dark Burnt Umber on a ¾-inch (19mm) wash. Add some highlight wood grain lines onto the rake with thinned lines of Flesh Tan on a no. 4 script liner.

Shade the clay pots down the left side and under the rims with a side-load float of Burnt Sienna on a ¾-inch (19mm) wash. Highlight the clay pots along the right side with a brush mix of Desert Sun Orange + a touch of White.

Paint thin raffia bows around the trunks of the trees with linework of Amethyst, followed with additional lines of Amethyst lightened with a touch of White on a no. 4 script liner.

The vining over the rake's tine is thin lines of Dark Burnt Umber. Paint the small one-stroke leaves along the vining with a double load of Dark Forest Green and Sea Grass on a no. 4 shader.

There are two blue birds on the floorcloth, one sitting on the tine of the rake and one on the top of the "L" shovel handle. Paint both in the same manner. First base the birds with a mix of Blue Velvet + White (1:1) on a no. 8 shader. Shade the birds' backs and the tops of their heads with a side-load float of Blue Velvet. Highlight the tummies with a side-load float of Paradise. Paint the tail and wing feathers with chisel-edge strokes of the dirty brush tipped into White. Paint the beaks with two small comma strokes (see page 10) of Spice Brown on a no. 1 Jackie Shaw liner. The eye is a dot of Black Green.

design tip

If you compare the completed floorcloth on the opposite page to the coordinated plaque, you'll see a few variations. When painting accessories, never feel you must stick rigidly to the same colors and detail as you used on the original. Explore the creative possibilities. Subtle differences might even make the coordinating pieces more interesting.

11 sponge corner highlighting

Use painter's masking tape to mask the four corners next to the border area. Side load a dampened round craft sponge into Moss Green and White, blend well on your palette and softly sponge highlighting in the corners to frame the design.

12 paint the border design

Paint a strokework design around the floor-cloth border using a brush mix of thinned Bahama Purple + Moss Green on a no. 8 shader. Using the same mix on a no. 4 script liner, paint a lifeline (see page 10) to separate the border from the field. Erase all visible pattern lines with a brown gum eraser and then varnish (see page 13).

A coordinating plaque for a door or vestibule table makes guests feel especially welcome. My plaque is custom cut, but item #14072 from Walnut Hollow Farm is similar.

easter eggs

Children love searching for Easter eggs. Now those eggs can be right under their feet, as pretty as can be! This floorcloth uses an egg-shaped tracing template, which can be used repeatedly without wearing it out. The egg-shaped template is so easy to use, you may want to try it on a variety of surfaces. How about a coordinating basket or tray?

materials

surface
Fredrix floorcloth canvas, 2' x 3' (61cm x 91cm)

brushes (Loew-Cornell)
Wash, series 7150 or 7550: ¾-inch (19mm),
1-inch (25mm) ~ Shader, series 7300:
nos. 8 &16 ~ Rake, series 7120: ¾-inch (19mm)
~ Liner, series 7350: no. 4 ~ Jackie Shaw liner,
series JS: no. 1 ~ Script liner, series 7050: no. 4

additional supplies
2- to 4-inch (51mm to 102mm) sponge roller ~
Quilter's ruler ~ Pencil ~ Masking tape ~ Tracing paper ~
Transfer paper and stylus ~ Card stock or thin cardboard,
about 4" x 5" (10cm x 13cm) ~ Brown gum eraser ~
Delta Ceramcoat Satin Interior Varnish ~ Large flat
or mop brush for varnishing

(the pattern for this floorcloth is on page 123)

colors
paint (Delta Ceramcoat)

blue mist	candlelight	white	paradise
coastline blue	village green	pale lilac	pink frosting
lilac	dark forest green	black green	aquamarine
spice tan	raspberry	antique rose	cape cod blue
paradise + white (1:1)	dark forest green + a touch of black green		

1 base, mark, begin plaid

Basecoat the floorcloth with Blue Mist, using a sponge roller. Let dry. Using a quilter's ruler and pencil, measure and mark a 4" (10cm) border all around the floorcloth. Mark another border 1" (25mm) wide to the inside of the 4" (10cm) border. Lay masking tape along the outer edges of the 1" (25mm) border and basecoat it with Candlelight, using a 1-inch (25mm) wash.

Begin the center plaid design with thinned White on a ¾-inch (19mm) rake. Paint each of the White stripes going in one direction with one long stroke. Let dry. Then, with the same long strokes, paint the White stripes in the opposite direction.

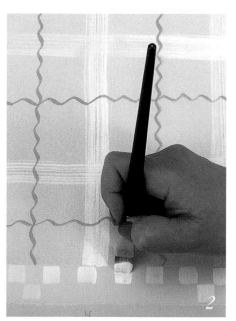

2 finish plaid, paint checks

Paint rick-rack lines between each plaid line, both horizontally and vertically, using a no. 4 script liner and thinned Paradise. Load a no. 16 shader with thinned White and freehand the checks (see page 12) around the Candlelight border area.

3 place egg shapes and basecoat

To create an egg template for tracing, transfer the egg pattern onto a piece of card stock or thin cardboard and then cut out the egg shape. Use your template and a pencil to trace egg shapes in clusters around the border. Basecoat the eggs in Candlelight, Coastline Blue, Village Green, Paradise + White (1:1), Pale Lilac and Pink Frosting. Some of these colors may need two coats to achieve opaque coverage. Let dry between basecoat layers. Erase any visible pencil lines around the Easter eggs with a brown gum eraser.

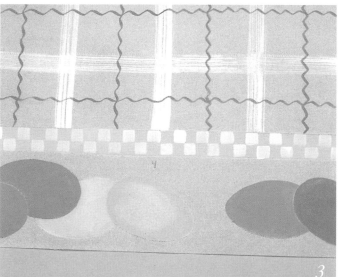

4 detail the pale lilac eggs

Using the no. 1 Jackie Shaw liner and Pink Frosting, detail each Pale Lilac egg with freehand curlicues. Let dry. Dampen with clear water the lower edges of these eggs and places where they tuck behind other eggs. Then shade with a side-load float of Lilac on a ¾-inch (19mm) wash.

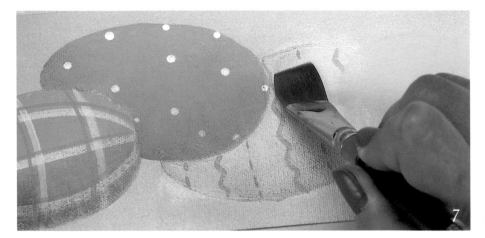

5 detail the village green eggs

Detail the Village Green eggs with a plaid design applied with a no. 4 liner. Start with thin horizontal White lines at the point of an egg and gently widen the lines as you paint across the egg's length. Curve the lines with the contour of the egg. These curved, thin-to-thick lines round out the egg. Paint curved vertical stripes across the horizontal. Let dry. Paint the blue plaid lines with thinned Paradise on a no. 4 script liner. Place them above and to the left of the White plaid lines. Shade the eggs with Dark Forest Green and a touch of Black Green in the same manner as you did in step 4.

6 detail the paradise + white eggs

Detail Paradise + White eggs with random White applied with the handle end of any brush. Let dry. Shade the eggs with Aquamarine in the same manner as you did in step 4.

7 detail the candlelight eggs

Detail the Candlelight eggs with zig-zag lines of Village Green painted with a no. 4 liner. In between the zig-zag lines, paint stitched lines of Paradise, using the same brush. Shade as described in step 4, using Spice Tan.

8 detail the pink frosting eggs

Paint the wide stripes and the hearts on the Pink Frosting eggs with thinned Raspberry, using a no. 8 shader for the bold stripes and a no. 4 liner for the hearts. To paint the hearts, stroke two little humps and then pull them down to a "V" to form the pointed bottom. Alternate the direction of the hearts to create a random look. Add a wiggly line to the outside edges of the bold stripes with thinned White on a no. 4 liner. Shade as described in step 4, using Antique Rose.

9 detail the coastline blue eggs

Paint a checked band through the middle of each Coastline Blue egg with thinned White and a no. 8 shader. Paint lifelines on both sides of the checked band with thinned Antique Rose on a no. 4 liner. Paint the random dots on the ends of the egg with Candlelight and the handle end of any brush. Shade as described in step 4, using Cape Cod Blue.

10 highlight eggs and finish border

Give the eggs roundness and help them stand out from the background by highlighting the top curves with a very sheer side-load float of White thinned with a little water on a ¾-inch (19mm) wash. Avoid highlighting any shaded areas. Finish the border of the floorcloth with a "stitching" line of thinned Lilac, painted with a no. 4 script liner (see photo below). Let the floorcloth dry completely and then varnish (see page 13).

field of daisies

This floorcloth, with it's sponged-on design, is perfect for children to paint—easy and fun. What a great gift this would be for Mother's Day or for a special neighbor. Also, this design is well-suited for a coordinating watering can, summer dinnerware, place mats, an apron, or stool tops.

colors
paint *(Delta Ceramcoat)*

coastline blue	candlelight	golden brown	white
burnt sienna	sunbright yellow	periwinkle blue	

materials

surface
Fredrix floorcloth canvas, 2' x 3' (61cm x 91cm)

brushes *(Loew-Cornell)*
Script liner, series 7050: no. 4

additional supplies
2- to 4-inch (51mm to 102mm) sponge roller ~ Tracing paper ~ Dark graphite paper and stylus ~ Sponge sheet, cut into pattern shapes ~ Delta Ceramcoat Satin Interior Varnish ~ Large flat or mop brush for varnishing

(patterns for this floorcloth are on page 122)

1 base, start yellow daisies

Basecoat the floorcloth with Coastline Blue and a sponge roller. Let dry. Transfer the pattern shapes onto a sponge sheet and cut them out (see page 13). Sponge yellow daisies at random over the floorcloth, using the petal-shaped sponge loaded into Candlelight. It's easiest to place each petal if you think of the daisy as the face of a clock: sponge the first petal at 12 o'clock, then sponge another petal at 6 o'clock, then another at 3 o'clock, then one at 9 o'clock. Leave space in the middle of each daisy to sponge in the flower center.

2 complete yellow daisies

Fill in between the main four petals with additional petals sponged at the 2, 4, 8, and 10 o'clock positions. As you place these yellow daisies at random over the field, leave room for the white daisies and allow some yellow daisies to extend over the outside edge of the floorcloth. Then, using a round-shaped sponge double loaded into Golden Brown and Candlelight, sponge in the flower center of each yellow daisy.

3 sponge white daisy petals

For the white daisies, load the petal-shaped sponge into White and stamp on the petals, using the same clock-face placement you used in steps 1 and 2. Let the white daisies overlap the yellow daisies, and let some white daisies extend over the outside edge of the floorcloth.

4 sponge white daisy centers

Double load the round sponge shape into Burnt Sienna and Sunbright Yellow. Sponge in the center of the white daisies.

5 outline white daisies

Outline around the petals of the white daisies, using White thinned with a little water and a no. 4 script liner. These outlines are painted freehand in a wiggly line.

6 sponge border

Finish the floorcloth with a border of blue "tiles" around the perimeter of the floorcloth. Using the square sponge loaded into Periwinkle Blue, apply one square in each corner of the floorcloth. Continue sponging squares along each side of the floorcloth from the corners toward the middle, allowing a little of the background to show between each tile. Adjust your spacing so the tiles don't overlap or leave a big gap in the middle. Reload the sponge with Periwinkle Blue as needed. Let the floorcloth dry completely and then varnish (see page 13).

To create an especially fresh look, accessorize your daisy floorcloth with a coordinated watering can you can fill with cut or silk daisies. Unpainted watering cans are available at hobby and craft stores.

flowers and bees

This floorcloth shouts Spring!—but it can be left out the entire summer also. You might even display it in winter as a reminder of warm, sunny weather and easy, breezy days to come. Whatever the season, this floorcloth would look great on a sun porch, in a bathroom or in a girl's cheery bedroom.

materials

surface

Fredrix floorcloth canvas, 2' x 3' (61cm x 91cm)

brushes (Loew-Cornell)

Wash, series 7150 or 7550: 1-inch (25mm) ~ Shader, series 7300: nos. 4, 8, 10, 12, 16 ~ Round stroke, series 7040: no. 8 ~ Deerfoot stippler, series 7850: ¼-inch (6mm) ~ Jackie Shaw liner, series JS: nos. 1, 2 ~ Script liner, series 7050: no. 10/0

additional supplies

2- to 4-inch (51mm to 102mm) sponge roller ~ Tracing paper ~ Dark graphite paper and stylus ~ Small round sponge ~ Pencil ~ Quilter's ruler ~ Brown gum eraser ~ Delta Ceramcoat Satin Interior Varnish ~ Large flat or mop brush for varnishing

(patterns for this floorcloth are on page 122)

colors
paint (Delta Ceramcoat)

coastline blue | medium foliage green | dark foliage green | light foliage green

wild rose | mulberry | peony | white

pale yellow | burnt sienna | passion | antique gold

periwinkle blue | opaque yellow | black

1 base, transfer, paint stems and leaves

Basecoat the entire cloth with Coastline Blue, using a sponge roller. Let dry. Transfer the flower patterns, putting flowers of different heights next to each other. Paint all flower stems with Medium Foliage Green, using a no. 1 Jackie Shaw liner. To paint the leaves, load a no. 12 shader with Medium Foliage Green, touching into Dark Foliage Green on one side for shading and Light Foliage Green on the other for high-lighting. Let the colors vary for interest. Most leaves are one-stroke leaves (see page 11) in various shapes. The leaves of the yellow-stroke flower (far right) are fine lines painted with Dark Foliage Green on a no. 1 Jackie Shaw liner.

2 paint the tulips

Base the tulip petals with Wild Rose, using a no. 12 shader. Shade with Mulberry at the tulip base and in a "V" shape at the bottom of the middle petal. Using a no. 2 Jackie Shaw liner and Peony, paint three strokes on the middle petal and three over-strokes of descending size on both side petals.

3 paint the daisies

Stroke in the daisy petals with White, using a no. 8 round stroke brush. Using the ¼-inch (6mm) deerfoot, stipple in the center with Pale Yellow. Working wet-on-wet, pick up a bit of Burnt Sienna on the longest bristles and stipple in shading at the bottom of the center. Also stipple a hollow in the center. Clean the brush and pick up a bit of White on the longest bristles. Stipple highlight at the top of the center and at the top of the hollow. With a stylus, place Burnt Sienna dots randomly around the center. Repeat with dots of Pale Yellow and then with dots of White.

deerfoot tip

The short bristles of the deerfoot brush are referred to as the "heel" and the long bristles as the "toe." Tap in the center of the daisies with a fully loaded deerfoot. Then touch the toe into the shade color. Stipple lightly on your palette to blend and then stipple on the shade areas of the center.

4 paint the purple flowers

To paint the purple flower petals, use petal strokes (see page 11) with a no. 12 shader double loaded with White into Passion. Outline the petals with Passion, using a no. 10/0 script liner. Using the wood end of the brush, loosely fill the centers with Pale Yellow dots. Add dots of Antique Gold at the bottom of the center and White dots at the top. With Medium Foliage Green and a no. 4 shader, add one-stroke leaf calyxes (see page 11) to the two buds.

5 paint the blue flowers

For the blue flower petals, double load a no. 16 shader with White into Periwinkle Blue and blend on the palette. Use the chisel petal stroke (see page 11). Lay one corner of a no. 10 shader into Pale Yellow and the other into Antique Gold. Do not blend. Create the flower centers with a series of chisel taps pivoting in a circle with the Pale Yellow to the center. Using the wood end of a small brush, add Pale Yellow dots in the very center.

6 paint yellow flowers and grass

The yellow flowers are comma strokes (see page 10) painted with a side-load float of Pale Yellow and a no. 8 shader. Using the wood end of a small brush, dot Wild Rose where the flowers connect to the stem.

Using a small round sponge and the three greens on your palette, lightly pounce along the base of all the flower stems. Loosely pull occasional grass blades with any of the greens, using a no. 1 Jackie Shaw liner. Using any colors on the palette and the wood end of a small brush, randomly dot in flowers along the grasses.

grass tip

When painting random grasses, as shown along the edge of this floorcloth, try turning your painting surface so you're pulling the grasses toward instead of away from you. This gives the grass a looser look and makes it seem more natural with the ends getting thinner.

7 add corner checks

With a pencil and quilter's ruler, mark guidelines for a 4" x 4" (10cm x 10cm) square of checks in each of the corners. With White on a 1-inch (25mm) wash, paint corner checks within these squares, starting with White at the corner point.

8 paint the bees

Transfer the bee pattern onto several places of the floorcloth. Base the bees with Pale Yellow, using a no. 4 shader. Shade the body and head on the side closest to the mat edge with Burnt Sienna. Highlight the opposite side of the bee with Opaque Yellow. The wings are White petal strokes painted with a side-loaded no. 8 shader. With a no. 10/0 script liner, paint the bee details—antennae, body stripes, stinger and bee path—with Black. Then paint a White shine line on the head and body. Allow the floorcloth to dry. Erase visible tracing lines with a brown gum eraser and then varnish (see page 13).

stars and stripes

What a perfect project for the Fourth of July! It's easy enough for you to do with your children or grandchildren. To create the stars, you have a choice between using star-shaped sponges or stencils—or both! Have fun making memories.

colors

paint *(Delta Ceramcoat)*

light ivory · cadet blue · opaque red

midnight blue · white

materials

surface

Fredrix floorcloth canvas, 2' x 3' (61cm x 91cm)

brushes *(Loew-Cornell)*

Script liner, series 7050: no. 1

additional supplies

2- to 4-inch (51mm to 102mm) sponge roller ~ Pencil ~ Quilter's ruler ~ Masking tape, 1½" (4cm) wide ~ Tracing paper ~ Sponge sheet (optional—see steps 2 and 4) ~ Dark graphite paper and stylus ~ A few paper towels ~ Rubber gloves (optional) ~ Star stencils, from about 2" (5cm) to 5" (13cm) diameter (optional—see steps 2 and 4) ~ Small round sponge ~ Brown gum eraser ~ Delta Ceramcoat Satin Interior Varnish ~ Large flat or mop brush for varnishing

(patterns for this floorcloth are on page 115)

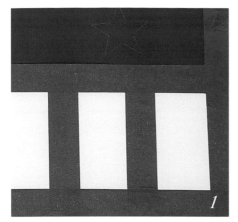

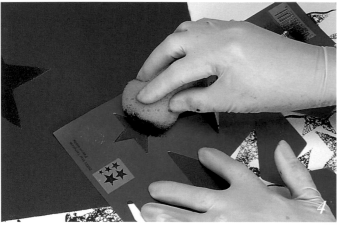

1 base and mask

Basecoat the entire cloth with Light Ivory, using a sponge roller. Let dry. With a quilter's ruler and pencil, mark off a 5" (13cm) border. Mask outside the inner panel with tape and then basecoat in Cadet Blue. Let dry. Remove the masking tape and then mask inside the blue panel on the short sides. On the long sides mask outside the blue panel running all the way to the edges of the mat. Find the middle of one of the short sides and, with a quilter's ruler, draw a guideline from the inner panel to the mat's edge. Center a strip of 1½" (4cm) masking tape along this line. Measure again for the midpoint between the center of this tape and the edge of the inner panel. Draw a guideline and lay a strip of masking tape as you did before. Do the same on the other side of the central strip. Follow the same masking process on the opposite short side. You should end up with four open sections on each short side.

2 sponge or stencil smaller red stars

The stars can be either sponged or stenciled, or you can use a combination of the two methods. This step describes the sponging process. Stenciling is described in step 4. Transfer the two smaller star shapes onto a sponge sheet and cut them out. Soak the sponge-sheet star shapes in water to expand. Squeeze out the excess water with a paper towel (see page 13). Dip the larger star into Opaque Red and apply two randomly spaced stars per taped-off section. Change to the smaller sponge star to loosely fill in the open areas. Let the star shapes overlap. Let dry and remove the tape.

Now repeat the masking procedure in step one for the long sides of the floorcloth. You should end with eight open sections on each side. Sponge in the red stars, let dry and remove the tape.

3 add corner stars and wavy lines

Using the largest star pattern, prepare a sponge as you did in step 2 (or you may use a stencil). Sponge a large Opaque Red star in each corner of the floorcloth. With a no. 1 script liner, draw an Opaque Red wavy line on either side of the red-star stripes. Then paint corner lines in Cadet Blue, starting the lines in the point of the corner.

4 begin stenciling center panel stars

You can usually find star stencils in craft or hobby stores, or you can make your own with plastic graph paper (see page 39). You will need several sizes. Position a star stencil in the center panel, load a small round sponge with Midnight Blue, and pounce in the star shape. Wipe off the stencil. Continue to pounce in stars in random positions and sizes, wiping off the stencil after each star. Alternatively, the stars in this and the next step can be sponged.

5 complete center panel stars, paint stitch lines

Clean your stencil and round sponge and let the Midnight Blue stars dry. Offset your stencil from the Midnight Blue stars and pounce in White stars of the same size on top of the blue stars. An edge of the Midnight Blue will remain on one side of the White stars to create a shadow. When you finish the White stars, you may want to touch up star edges with the no. 1 script liner. For the last touch, paint White stitching lines around the inner panel, ½" (13mm) from the panel edge. Allow the floorcloth to dry thoroughly, erase any visible pencil lines with a brown gum eraser and then varnish (see page 13).

Patriotism isn't just for July. You may want to keep your Stars and Stripes floorcloth out through the year—and you'll find dozens of uses for this coordinating Shaker box (item RB56 from Hall's Woodcrafts).

spooky night

Even though the Halloween season is fairly short, it offers almost irresistible decorating possibilities. This design has everything you need to create the right scary atmosphere—ghosts, haunted houses, gravestones, bats and lurking eyes. What fun to have this floorcloth inside your door for your Halloween guests to see.

colors
paint *(Delta Ceramcoat)*

nightfall blue	charcoal	cape cod blue	blue storm
blue velvet	calypso orange	dark goldenrod	opaque yellow
gamal green	black green	light timberline green	mustard
spice brown	black	mudstone	drizzle grey
white	tangerine	burnt sienna	medium foliage green

materials

surface
Fredrix floorcloth canvas, 2' x 3' (61cm x 91cm)

brushes *(Loew-Cornell)*
Wash, series 7150 or 7550: 1-inch (25mm) ~ Shader, series 7300: nos. 4, 6, 8, 12, 20 ~ Jackie Shaw liner, series JS: nos. 1, 2 ~ Script liner, series 7050: nos. 10/0, 1

additional supplies
2- to 4-inch (51mm to 102mm) sponge roller ~ Pencil ~ Quilter's ruler ~ Tracing paper ~ Light transfer paper and stylus ~ Brown gum eraser ~ Delta Ceramcoat Satin Interior Varnish ~ Large flat or mop brush for varnishing

(pattern for this floorcloth is on pages 124-125)

1 base, transfer, drybrush and shade sky

Basecoat the floorcloth with Nightfall Blue and a sponge roller. With a quilter's ruler and pencil, mark off a border line 5" (13cm) from the edges of the cloth. Basecoat outside the line in Charcoal with a 1-inch (25mm) wash. Transfer the pattern except for the gate, the fence, the gravestones, the pumpkins and the portion of the house inside the moon. Drybrush the sky with Cape Cod Blue and then with Blue Storm, using a 1-inch (25mm) wash. Shade the sky in the floorcloth corners and the area next to the moon with a side-load float of Blue Velvet.

2 paint moon, grass and path

Basecoat the moon with Calypso Orange, using a 1-inch (25mm) wash. While the moon is still wet, shade the bottom with Dark Goldenrod and highlight the top with Opaque Yellow. Basecoat the grass in Gamal Green with a no. 20 shader. Before the grass dries, streak Black Green shading upward from the bottom of the hills and streak highlighting downward from the tops of the hills with Light Timberline Green and touches of Mustard. Paint the path with streaks of Spice Brown, using a no. 8 shader. Shade the sides of the path with a side load of Black. Lightly streak Mudstone through the path. Keep all streaks parallel to the horizon. Let dry and transfer the rest of the pattern.

3 paint and shadow the house

Basecoat the house with Black and a no. 8 shader. Use a no. 1 Jackie Shaw liner for the porch rails. Highlight the roof shingles, down the edges of the house sections, inside the windows and the door edges with a no. 1 Jackie Shaw liner loaded in Black and tipped in Mudstone. Use a no. 10/0 script liner to paint the window details, spiderwebs and cats. With a no. 8 shader, lightly streak a Black shadow on the grass in front of the house.

4 add trees and their shadows

Paint the trees with Black. Use a no. 2 Jackie Shaw liner for the trunks and a no. 1 Jackie Shaw liner for the finer branches, pulling them over the moon for effect. Use either liner to add texture to the trunk with touches of Mudstone. With Black on a no. 8 shader, streak shadows below the tree trunks. For the trees to the left of the moon, the shadows fall to the left. For trees to the right of the moon, the shadows fall to the right.

5 paint bats and gravestones

With the no. 1 Jackie Shaw liner, paint bats against the sky and the moon by making a middle dot with a wing on each side. Using a no. 6 shader, basecoat gravestones in Mudstone. Shade with Black along the bottom and right side and highlight top and left side with Drizzle Grey. Paint gravestone shadows with streaks of Black and a no. 6 shader. Gravestone lettering is done with Black and a no. 10/0 script liner.

6 paint and shadow the gate

Paint the gate and fence with Black and highlight with touches of Drizzle Grey and with White, using the no. 1 Jackie Shaw liner.

Switching to the no. 8 shader, streak in a bit of shadowing under the gate with Black.

7 paint the pumpkins

Basecoat the pumpkins in Dark Goldenrod with a no. 8 shader. Paint the section edges and outer edges of the pumpkin with a side-load float of Tangerine. Shade the separations again with Spice Brown. Shade along the bottoms of the pumpkins and between the pumpkins with Burnt Sienna. Paint the facial features with a 10/0 script liner. Use Black for the openings and outline with Calypso Orange—sometimes reversing these colors. Using a no. 4 shader, paint the stems in Spice Brown. Then shade in Black and highlight with a brush mix of Spice Brown + White. Vines and leaves are Black, painted with a no. 1 Jackie Shaw liner.

8 paint ghosts and eyeballs

Paint the ghosts with a no. 12 shader and very thin, sheer White. Reinforce the edges with a side-load float of White. Using a no. 1 Jackie Shaw liner, paint the facial features in Black and outline with White. Add a White highlight dot to the eyes.

Using a no. 4 shader, basecoat the faceless eyeballs with two coats of Opaque Yellow and shade with Medium Foliage Green at the bottoms of the eyeballs. Add Black pupils. Dot in a White highlight at the tops of the pupils and a Medium Foliage Green comma-stroke (see page 10) to create a highlight the bottom of the pupils.

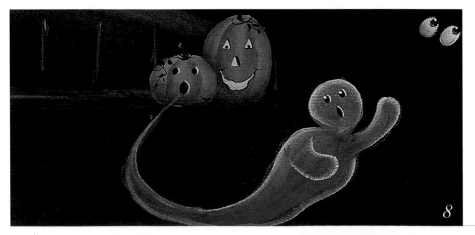

9 add border checks and lifeline

Paint two rows of checks at each corner with Tangerine, using a no. 12 shader (see page 12). Make the checks darkest at the corner points and let them fade as they progress in both directions along the sides. Using a no. 1 script liner, draw a line of Opaque Yellow all around the mat, ¼" (6mm) from the edge. Allow the floorcloth to dry thoroughly. Erase any visible tracing lines with a brown gum eraser and then varnish (see page 13).

shadow tip

To create shadows under an object, use the brush chisel edge to streak the shadow under that object. Remember two things: have the shadow color just touch the object and pull all shadows in the same area the same direction. On this floorcloth, the moon is the light source, so pull all shadows away from the moon.

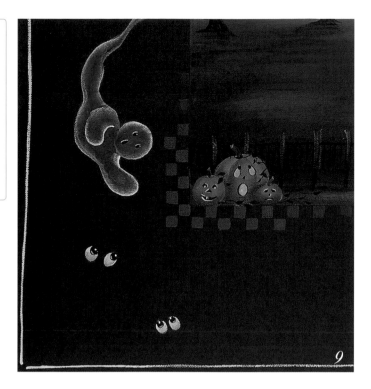

autumn leaves

This is a great floorcloth for celebrating autumn without getting into specific holidays. You can keep it out from September through November. The colors fit well with many of today's decorating trends. What's more, you'll find the sponging technique used for the autumn leaves is fun and easy.

materials

surface
Fredrix floorcloth canvas, 2' x 3' (61cm x 91cm)

brushes *(Loew-Cornell)*
Wash, series 7150 or 7550, ½-inch (13mm),
¾-inch ~ (19mm), 1-inch (25mm) ~
Script liner, series 7050: nos. 10/0, 4

additional supplies
Pencil ~ Quilter's ruler ~ Toothbrush ~
Tracing paper ~ Dark transfer paper and stylus ~
Sponge sheet ~ Scissors ~ Tub of clean water
~ A few paper towels ~ Brown gum eraser ~
Delta Ceramcoat Satin Interior Varnish
~ Large flat or mop brush for varnishing

(the patterns for this floorcloth are on page 123)

colors
paint *(Delta Ceramcoat)*

trail tan	autumn brown	burnt umber	dark burnt umber
raw linen	english yew green	light timberline green	lemon grass
burnt sienna	straw	spice tan	red iron oxide
georgia clay	spice brown	straw + light timberline green (1:1)	trail tan + spice tan + english yew green (4:1:1)

flyspecking tip

Flyspecking can be done several ways. Two are described in this book, one on page 12 and the other on page 113 (step 7). Try both and see which you like best—or use use another method that you prefer.

1 base, shade border, flyspeck

Basecoat the entire cloth with Trail Tan, using a sponge roller. With a pencil and quilter's ruler, mark off a 4" (10cm) border. Shade the outside of the border with a float of Autumn Brown, using a 1-inch (25mm) wash, going darker at the corners. Using the same brush, shade the inside of the upper left and lower right corners with Burnt Umber. Mask the outside shading at these corners with paper and flyspeck with Autumn Brown, fading out toward the opposite corner. Repeat with Burnt Umber.

2 pull and overstroke branch

Load a no. 4 script liner with a brush mix of Burnt Umber + Dark Burnt Umber and pull a freehand branch. While the paint is still wet, make slightly curved overstrokes across the branch, using Raw Linen and a ½-inch (13mm) wash. The brush should barely touch the surface, just skimming over the dark background to create a bark effect .

3 add tendrils

Using a no. 10/0 script liner, add tendrils in Dark Burnt Umber.

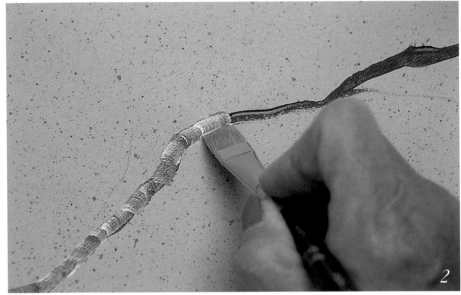

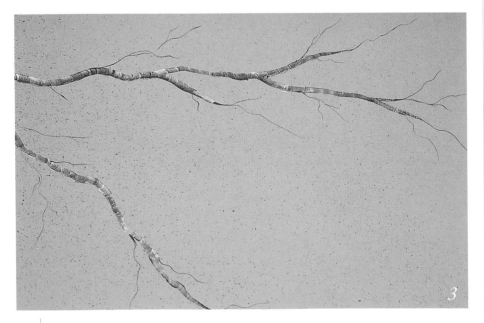

4 cut out sponge leaves, sponge on green leaves

Transfer the leaf shapes onto a sponge sheet. Cut out the leaves and dampen them in a tub of water to expand the sponges. Squeeze out the excess moisture with a paper towel. Lightly load one of the green leaf sponges into English Yew Green. Then tip one side into Light Timberline Green and the other side into Lemon Grass. Pounce the loaded sponge two or three times on a paper towel to remove excess paint. Then touch the leaf sponge on the floorcloth where you want a leaf to appear. Add more green leaves, using all three green-leaf sponges. Let dry.

5 add shading, highlighting and veins

Shade the green leaves with side-load floats of Burnt Sienna using a ½-inch (13mm) wash. Highlight with Straw and Straw + Light Timberline Green (1:1) Add center veins and side veins with Dark Burnt Umber, using a 10/0 script liner.

6 sponge on the oak leaves

For the oak leaves, double load one of the oak-leaf sponges with Spice Tan and Straw. Pounce the loaded sponge two or three times on a paper towel to remove excess paint. Then touch the leaf sponge on the floorcloth where you want an oak leaf to appear. Add more oak leaves, using both of the oak leaf sponges. Let dry.

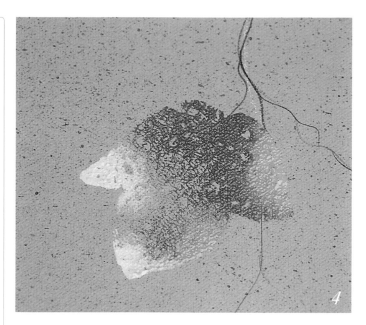

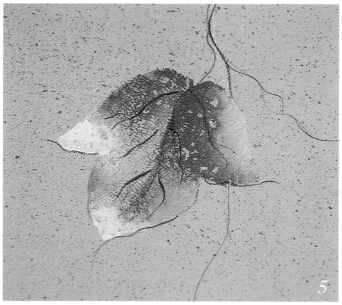

sponge tip

Once you've expanded your cut-out sponge, squeeze out the excess water well. A paper towel helps, because it really soaks up the water. Using a too-damp sponge could result in paint bleeding out on the edges.

7 add oak leaf tints and veins

Using the ½-inch (13mm) wash, tint some of the oak leaf edges, using Burnt Sienna, Red Iron Oxide and English Yew Green randomly. Do the same along the center vein areas. Add center veins and side veins with Dark Burnt Umber on a 10/0 script liner.

8 sponge on the maple leaves

Lightly dip one of the maple leaf sponges into Spice Tan. Add Red Iron Oxide on one side and Georgia Clay on the other. Pounce the loaded sponge two or three times on a paper towel to remove excess paint. Then touch the leaf sponge on the floorcloth where you want a maple leaf to appear. Add more maple leaves, using both of the maple leaf sponges. Let dry.

9 add maple leaf tints and veins

Using the ½-inch (13mm) wash, tint some of the maple leaf edges, using Burnt Sienna, Straw and English Yew Green randomly. Do the same along the center vein area. Add center veins and side veins with Dark Burnt Umber on a no. 10/0 script liner.

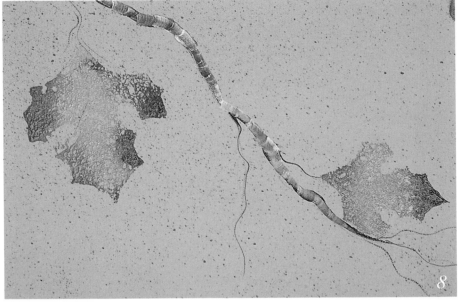

wash vs. tint tip

A wash is a a very sheer covering of paint. A tint is a very sheer side-load float of color along an edge or wherever else it is called for.

10 stroke in shadow leaves

Using a ³/₄-inch (19mm) wash, brush-mix Trail Tan + Spice Tan + English Yew Green(4:1:1), thinned with water, and paint shadow leaves. These are random one-stroke leaves (see page 11) along the branches.

11 sponge a maple leaf border

Load the small maple leaf sponge with Spice Tan and then the stem end with Spice Brown. Pick up Straw or Georgia Clay or Red Iron Oxide on the tip or side of the sponge. Pounce on a paper towel and then sponge the leaf onto the border. Continue to sponge border leaves, varying the tip and side colors randomly. Add trail twigs, center veins and side veins with Dark Burnt Umber on a script 10/0 liner. Allow the floorcloth to dry thoroughly. Erase visible pattern lines with a brown gum eraser and and then varnish (see page 13).

This tray enhances any autumn occasion, whether used to hold treats or simply to add a warm decorative note. The tray I used is an old one I'd had for years. Check out your own kitchen, flea markets or craft shops for a similar surface.

sweet treats

Floorcloth canvas can also be used to create a table runner. Imagine this piece on your dining room table, sideboard cabinet or kitchen island for a holiday buffet. Topped with both real and painted sweet treats galore, your runner will be especially appealing to your family and guests. And when your entertaining is done, you'll find cleanup a snap.

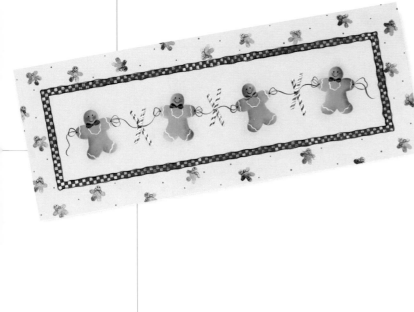

materials

surface

Fredrix floorcloth canvas, 2' x 3' (61cm x 91cm), cut to 14" x 36" (36cm x 91cm)

brushes (Loew-Cornell)

Wash, series 7150 or 7550: ¾-inch (19mm) ~ Shader, series 7300: nos. 4, 8 ~ Mop, series 275: 1-inch (25mm) ~ Jackie Shaw liner, series JS: no. 1

additional supplies

2- to 4-inch (51mm to 102mm) sponge roller ~ Pencil ~ Quilter's ruler ~ Tracing paper ~ Grey graphite paper and stylus ~ Sponge sheet ~ Scissors ~ Tub of clean water ~ A few paper towels ~ Brown gum eraser ~ Delta Ceramcoat Satin Interior Varnish ~ Large flat or mop brush for varnishing

(stencil patterns for this table runner are on page 123)

colors
paint (Delta Ceramcoat)

raw linen	opaque red	latte	white
autumn brown	spice brown	flesh tan	chocolate cherry
perfect highlight for red	ocean reef blue	blue storm	caribbean blue
christmas green	black green	perfect highlight for green	burnt umber
midnight blue			

1 basecoat, transfer patterns

Basecoat the entire floorcloth canvas with Raw Linen and a sponge roller. Use a pencil and quilter's ruler to measure and mark a 2½" (6cm) border. Measure and mark a ½" (13mm) border inside the first border and basecoat it with Opaque Red. Transfer the large gingerbread man and peppermint stick patterns onto the center field. You should have four gingerbread men alternating with three pairs of peppermint sticks. Basecoat the large gingerbread men with Latte and the peppermint sticks with White.

2 shade gingerbread men

Sideload a ¾" (19mm) wash with Autumn Brown. To shade and add roundness to the gingerbread men, apply a side-load float along one side of each head and down one side of each body.

3 detail the gingerbread men

Dampen with clean water the areas around the gingerbread men and then float in background shadows, using Spice Brown sparingly side loaded onto a ¾-inch (19mm) wash. Use a dry 1-inch (25mm) mop to soften the shadows and fade them into the background.

Highlight one side of each gingerbread man with a soft side-load float of Flesh Tan on a ¾-inch (19mm) wash.

Basecoat the bow ties on the two end gingerbread men with Opaque Red on a no. 4 shader. Shade the center knot and the loops of their bow ties with a side-load float of Chocolate Cherry and a no. 8 shader. Highlight the loops of the bow ties and the top of the knots with a side-load float of Perfect Highlight for Red and a no. 8 shader. One of the "inner" gingerbread men has a blue bow tie and the other has a green. The blue bow tie is basecoated with Ocean Reef Blue, shaded with Blue Storm and highlighted with Caribbean Blue. The green bow tie is basecoated with Christmas Green, shaded with Black Green and highlighted with Perfect Highlight for Green.

Dampen the gingerbread men's cheeks with clean water and then add blush to the cheeks with a soft side-load float of thinned Opaque Red on a no. 8 shader.

The wavy icing lines are painted with thinned White on a no. 1 Jackie Shaw liner. The eyes, mouth, and dots on the ends of the arms are Burnt Umber.

Reinforce the Autumn Brown shading you did in step 2. This will set the icing on the surface of the gingerbread men.

4 base the peppermint stick stripes

The widest stripes on the peppermint sticks are painted as S-strokes (see page 10), using the no. 4 shader. Basecoat the red stripes in Opaque Red and the green stripes in Christmas Green. Paint the thin stripes with a no. 1 Jackie Shaw liner, using Opaque Red on the green peppermint sticks and thinned Ocean Reef Blue on the red peppermint sticks.

5 shade and highlight peppermints, paint ribbon

Shade one outside edge of each peppermint stick and the area where two sticks cross each other with a very sheer side-load float of Midnight Blue and a no. 8 shader. Highlight down the middle of each peppermint stick with a strong, hit-and-miss line of White and a no. 1 Jackie Shaw liner. Paint the ribbon connecting the peppermint sticks and gingerbread men as a line of Opaque Red applied with a no. 1 Jackie Shaw liner.

6 sponge gingerbread men on the border

Now you're ready to sponge small gingerbread men on the white border (see "Sponge Shape Stippling" on page 13). Double load the sponge with Latte and Autumn Brown. Blend the colors by pouncing the sponge on the palette before stamping the gingerbread men at random on the border. Vary the directions of the gingerbread men.

sponge tip

For evenly sponged shapes, pounce your loaded sponge onto a waxed palette at least ten times to blend the color well into the sponge.

7 paint gingerbread men and border detail

Detail the sponged gingerbread men with linework bow ties of Opaque Red, Christmas Green and Ocean Reef Blue, painted with a no. 1 Jackie Shaw liner. Paint the eyes as dots of Burnt Umber.

Paint random polka dots in the white border with the handle end of any paintbrush and Ocean Reef Blue.

Detail the red border area with a checked pattern, using a no. 8 shader and thinned White. Paint the corner checks first, continuing in both directions until the checks meet in the middle of the sides (see page 12). Outline both edges of the red border with wavy lifelines of thinned Christmas Green, painted with a no. 1 Jackie Shaw liner. Let the paint dry completely. Erase all visible pattern lines with a brown gum eraser and then varnish (see page 13).

happy holly days

You can't help but appreciate the versatility of this floorcloth. The half-moon can be used in so many areas—in front of your fireplace, inside a door, in front of a counter. What's more, the classic holly design goes with many holiday decorating themes. This half-moon, or semicircle, shape is precut by Fredrix, so you don't have to worry about cutting a perfect curve.

materials

surface
Fredrix floorcloth canvas, semicircle, 36" (91cm) length

brushes (Loew-Cornell)
Wash, series 7150 or 7550: ½-inch (13mm) ~ Shader, series 7300: nos. 4, 10 ~ Jackie Shaw liner, series JS: no. 1 ~ Script liner, series 7050: no. 1

additional supplies
2- to 4-inch (51mm to 102mm) sponge roller ~ Pencil ~ Quilter's ruler ~ Tracing paper ~ Dark graphite paper and stylus ~ Soapstone pencil ~ Brown gum eraser ~ Delta Ceramcoat Satin Interior Varnish ~ Large flat or mop brush for varnishing

(patterns for this floorcloth are on page 125)

colors
paint *(Delta Ceramcoat)*

antique white

deep river green

black green

kelly green

lime green

perfect highlight for green

moroccan red

black cherry

perfect highlight for red

green isle

lime green + kelly green (2:1)

lime green + green isle (2:1)

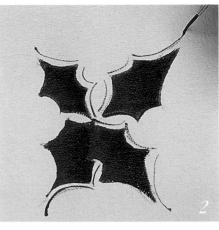

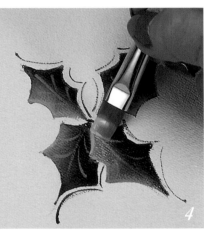

1 base and transfer

Basecoat the cloth with Antique White, using a sponge roller. Let dry. Mark off with a pencil and quilter's ruler two lines around the cloth, 3" (8cm) and 4" (10cm) from the edge. Transfer the holly pattern, repeating the design with random placement in the central portion of the mat. Basecoat the 3" (8cm) border with Deep River Green. Basecoat the holly leaves with Deep River Green and a no. 10 shader. Apply two coats.

2 shade and outline leaves

Shade the side of the leaves toward the curve of the floorcloth with Black Green, using a no. 10 shader. Outline the shade side of the leaves with the same color on a no. 1 Jackie Shaw liner.

3 highlight leaves

Highlight the other side of the leaves with Kelly Green, using a no. 10 shader. Strengthen with Lime Green, as you see on the top two leaves in this cluster.

4 paint veins and rehighlight

Paint the veins with a brush mix of Lime Green and Kelly Green (2:1), using a no. 1 Jackie Shaw liner. Rehighlight small areas of the leaves where you want them to be the lightest with Perfect Highlight for Green, using the no. 10 shader. These lightest highlights are particularly important where one leaf overlaps another.

5 paint berries

Base the berries with Moroccan Red, using a no. 4 shader. Shade the side of the berries where they come together with a side-load float of Black Cherry. Highlight the outside edges of the berries with a float of Perfect Highlight for Red.

6 add border checks

Starting in the corners of the inner 1" (25mm) border and working both ends toward the middle, paint the checks with Moroccan Red using a ½-inch (13mm) wash (see page 12).

7 paint scrolls and strokework

Use a quilter's ruler and soapstone pencil to mark off 4" (10cm) increments in the middle of the 3" (8cm) border. These increments indicate each strokework section. Pull the line scrolls with Lime Green + Green Isle (2:1), using a no. 1 script liner. Load a no. 10 shader with Kelly Green, tip with Lime Green and add the strokework.

8 dot along scrolls

Dot along the scrollwork lines with Moroccan Red on the wood tip of a no. 1 Jackie Shaw liner. Start at the base of the scrolled line and let the dots get smaller as the paint is used up. Reload each time you move to a new scrollwork section. Allow the floorcloth to dry thoroughly. Erase any visible pattern lines with a brown gum eraser and then varnish (see page 13).

Can't you just see a selection of Christmas cookies on this plate! The coordinating floorcloth and serving piece (item P-120 from Wayne's Woodenware) are sure to add to holiday cheer.

midnight snowfall

Snowflakes are the lovely art of nature. Celebrate the beauty and wonder of winter with this fun and easy-to-paint snowflake sampler floorcloth, featuring four types of painted snowflakes—stenciled, star-like, linework and flyspecked. You can create variations of the snowflake design with these methods, so, as in nature, no two of your snowflakes need be alike.

colors
paint *(Delta Ceramcoat)*

midnight blue

periwinkle blue

coastline blue

white

materials
surface
Fredrix floorcloth canvas, 2' x 3' (61cm x 91cm)

brushes *(Loew-Cornell)*
Rake, series 7120: ³/₄-inch (19mm)
~ Jackie Shaw liner, series JS: no. 1

additional supplies
2- to 4-inch (51mm to 102mm) sponge roller ~ Pencil ~ Quilter's ruler ~ Masking tape ~ Round craft sponge ~ Delta Holiday Snowflakes Pre-cut Stencil, #95-638 ~ Tracing paper ~ Light transfer paper and stylus ~ Brown gum eraser ~ Delta Ceramcoat Satin Interior Varnish ~ Large flat or mop brush for varnishing

(patterns for the floorcloth are on page 123)

1 base, sponge border edge

Basecoat the entire floorcloth with Midnight Blue and a sponge roller. Measure and tape off a 1½" (4cm) border around the floor-cloth. Using a round craft sponge loaded into Periwinkle Blue, softly sponge the border area next to the tape. Apply the paint stronger next to the tape and then let it fade out as it moves toward the floor-cloth edge. Remove the tape before the paint dries completely. Let dry.

2 stencil snowflake

Before painting any snowflakes, read through the snowflake tips below. Then, using a snowflake stencil and a round craft sponge, dab in Periwinkle Blue snowflakes randomly spaced over the floorcloth field. To enhance the look of a natural snowfall, stencil your snowflakes in a variety of sizes.

snowflake tips

*1)*Go for a "random" or unpredictable placement of snowflakes. To help achieve this look, think of triangles with different length sides. Place three snowflakes on the point of these triangles (see drawing on the right). *2)*Start with the largest snowflake style first. *3)*Strive for different values of brightness—let some snowflakes be less important, fading into the background. *4)*When stenciling snowflakes, you may want to tape off areas of the stencil not in use to prevent accidental paint spots.

imaginary triangles

Imaginary triangles can help you create a random look as you place your snowflakes.

3 detail the stenciled snowflakes

Accent the left side of each of the largest snowflakes' "arms" with a line of Coastline Blue and a no. 1 Jackie Shaw liner. Further detail some stenciled snowflakes with dots of Coastline Blue painted with the brush tip of the liner.

4 paint the star-like snowflakes

Paint the star-like snowflakes on areas dampened with clear water. Place a dot of White onto the wet surface and allow it to bleed into the background. Let dry. Pull rays out of the dot of White with thinned Coastline Blue and a no. 1 Jackie Shaw liner.

5 paint the linework snowflakes

Paint the linework snowflakes using a no. 1 Jackie Shaw liner and thinned Coastline Blue. You can use the patterns on page 123 or improvise your own snowflake designs. Start with six fine lines to define the snowflake. Using the same color and brush, detail these six lines by adding short branching lines. Also add short lines coming out from the center, using the same color and brush. Further detail the snowflakes with dots of White painted with the brush tip of the no. 1 Jackie Shaw liner.

6 scatter and vary styles

Scatter a variety of all the snowflake styles over the floorcloth, letting some "escape" into the border area.

7 flyspeck entire floorcloth

Complete your painting by flyspecking, or spattering, snowflakes over the entire floorcloth. To do this, load soupy White onto a ¾-inch (19mm) rake. Then tap the rake over the handle of another brush while holding both brushes over the floorcloth. The more water you add to the paint, the larger the spatter dots will be. Let the floorcloth dry completely. Erase any visible pattern lines and then varnish (see page 13).

flyspecking tip

Flyspecking can also be done
with a toothbrush. This method
is explained on page 12.

patterns

colonial village on sisal

These patterns may be hand-traced or photocopied for personal use only. Enlarge at 200 percent to bring up to full size.

black and white toile

These patterns may be hand-traced or photocopied for personal use only. Enlarge at 200 percent and enlarge again at 111% to bring up to full size. The relative positions of the flower groups are not to scale. Transfer each group separately, using the diagram on this page and the photo of the completed floorcloth on page 49 to help determine placement.

Use diamond pattern for border.

red roses

red five-petal

bell flowers

blue bell flowers

red roses

red five-petal

blue daisy

red berries

blue four-petal

red berries

french country

These patterns may be hand-traced or photocopied for personal use only. Enlarge at 200 percent to bring up to full size.

blue daisies

red five-petal

red berries

red five-petal

blue daisies

red five-petal

blue strokes

These patterns may be hand-traced or photocopied for personal use only. Enlarge at 200 percent to bring up to full size.

tone-on-tone strokes

This pattern may be hand-traced or photocopied for personal use only. Enlarge at 200 percent to bring up to full size.

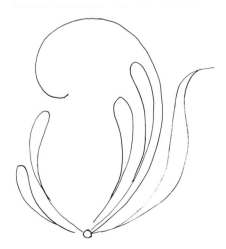

heart of the home

These patterns may be hand-traced or photocopied for personal use only. Enlarge at 200 percent to bring up to full size.

garden welcome

This pattern may be hand-traced or photocopied for personal use only. Enlarge at 200 percent and enlarge again at 107% to bring up to full size.

flowers and bees

These patterns may be hand-traced or photocopied for personal use only. Enlarge at 200 percent to bring up to full size.

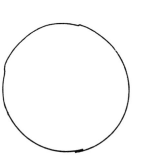

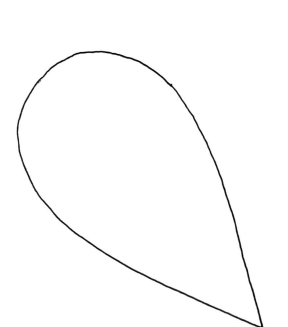

field of daisies

These patterns may be hand-traced or photocopied for personal use only. The patterns are full size.

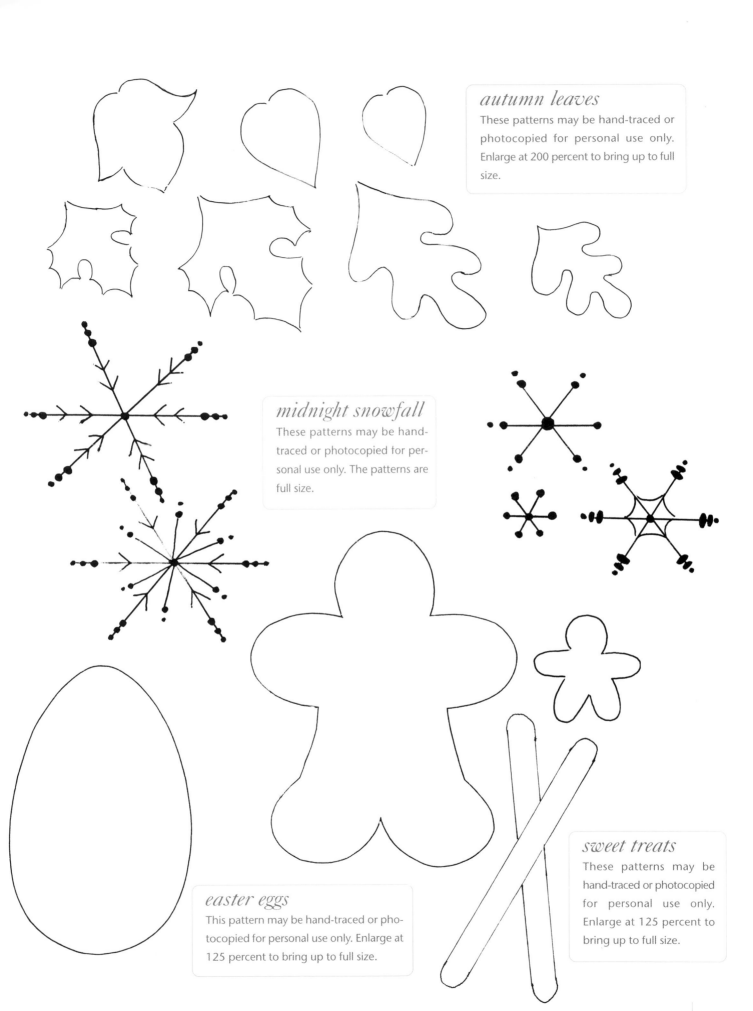

autumn leaves

These patterns may be hand-traced or photocopied for personal use only. Enlarge at 200 percent to bring up to full size.

midnight snowfall

These patterns may be hand-traced or photocopied for personal use only. The patterns are full size.

easter eggs

This pattern may be hand-traced or photocopied for personal use only. Enlarge at 125 percent to bring up to full size.

sweet treats

These patterns may be hand-traced or photocopied for personal use only. Enlarge at 125 percent to bring up to full size.

spooky night

This pattern may be hand-traced or photocopied for personal use only. Enlarge at 200 percent, then enlarge again at 135 percent to bring up to full size.